CRAFT BOOK

Reproducible Craft Pages for Preschool and Elementary Students!

See our Special HomeLink Activities!

Noah's Park® Children's Church Craft Book (Green Edition)

Product Developer:	Karen Pickering
Managing Editor:	Doug Schmidt
Editor:	Judy Gillispie
Contributing Writers:	René Stewart Diane Cory Nancy Sutton Karen Schmidt Gail Rohlfing
Craft Facilitator:	Judie Tippie
Interior Design:	Mike Riester
Cover Design:	Todd Mock
Illustrations:	Aline Heiser Chris Sharp

Published by Cook Communications Ministries
4050 Lee Vance View · Colorado Springs, CO 80918-7100
www.cookministries.com

Printed in Canada.

ISBN: 0-7814-3843-8   101795

TABLE OF CONTENTS

Unit 5 *God Made Us*

Unit 6 *We Worship God Together*

Unit 7 *Jesus Shows His Love and Greatness*

Unit 8 *Jesus and His Friends Show His Love*

INTRODUCTION

The crafts included in this book coordinate with each lesson in the Noah's Park Leader's Guide. Each craft activity is designed to help reinforce the Bible story the children have heard and participated in during the lesson. The craft is also designed to help the children and their parents extend the learning even further by linking it to activities they can do at home during the following week.

If a craft is to be cut out and put together, be sure to include the HomeLink by gluing it to the back of the craft, enclosing it in a resealable plastic bag, or attaching it in some other way to be sent home.

You will notice the designation for the activities. **GCE** refers to the Elementary Craft in the Green Edition of Noah's Park Children's Church. **GCP** refers to the Preschool Craft in the Green Edition of the Noah's Park Children's Church. The number following that designation identifies the lesson number.

Each craft activity has a list of supplies listed which you will want to gather prior to your session. You may want to make one of the crafts in advance so that you can show the children what they will make. This will also assist the Park Patrol members as they help the children.

There are some basic supplies that you should keep on hand. These are listed below. Other supplies are more specialized and should be gathered as needed.

Pencils with erasers

Markers

Drawing Paper

Construction Paper (variety of colors, both 9 " x 12 " and 12 " x 18 ")

Tape

Glue, paste, or glue sticks

Scissors

Craft Sticks

Paper fasteners, paper clips

Stapler and staples

Yarn, glitter, confetti

Resealable plastic bags (sandwich size)

GCE1: Hidden Message

Supplies: A copy of this craft page for each child · Orange, red, green and blue markers or crayons

Directions: There's a message hidden on this page! Can you find it? Get some crayons or markers, then use the code below to color the spaces and figure it out!

HomeLink: Today we learned that we are important to Jesus. Retell the Bible story about Nathanael to your family. Then all during the week remind each other that you are all important to Jesus! Hang up your Hidden Message as a reminder to all your family members of your importance to Jesus.

O = Orange   R = Red   G = Green   B = Blue

GCP1: Bible Story Puppets

Supplies: Crayons or washable markers · Scissors · Craft sticks (4 per child) · Tape · Resealable plastic bags

Preparation: Make a copy of the craft sheet for each child. You may want to cut out the puppets before class if your students are too young to cut.

Directions: Have the children color the figures of Jesus, Nathanael, and Philip. If the figures are not already cut out, have the children do that now. Help the children tape a craft stick to the back of each figure to make a handle for the puppets. Write the children's names on the backs of their puppets. Place each child's puppets and the "HomeLink" in a resealable plastic bag to send home.

HomeLink: (John 1:43-49) Use the puppets to help your child retell the Bible story at home this week.

Jesus asked Philip to be His helper. Have your child hold the Jesus and Philip puppets.

Philip went to tell his friend Nathanael. Have your child set down the Jesus puppet and pick up Nathanael.

Nathanael went with Philip to meet Jesus. Hold the Jesus puppet for your child.

Nathanael was surprised that Jesus knew all about him. Have the Jesus puppet nod yes.

Nathanael knew that Jesus was God's Son. Have your child make the Nathanael puppet nod yes.

Nathanael became one of Jesus' helpers too. Take all three puppets and have them pretend to travel.

Jesus

Nathanael

Philip

GCE2: Cana Maze

Supplies: Copy of the Cana Maze for each child · Pencils · Brown yarn · Glue · Crayons or markers

Preparation: Make one copy of the Cana Maze for each child. Cut yarn into pieces 24 inches long, one for each child.

Directions: Help the king's officer find Jesus! Use a pencil to trace the path from Capernaum to Cana. Then glue a piece of brown yarn over the path to show the dirt road. Color the rest of the picture.

HomeLink: The king's officer needed help! His son was very, very sick. Who did the he ask for help? Jesus! Did Jesus help him? Yes! Do you ever have problems? You can ask Jesus for help, too. Jesus loves for you to talk with Him. Jesus wants to help you. Set up a time to pray with your family about any problems you may face.

GCP2: Jesus Loves Me Necklaces

Supplies: Copy of the necklace pieces and Home Story for each child · Washable markers · Scissors · Glue · Hole punch · Yarn or lanyard cord · Cardboard or craft fun foam · Resealable bags · Optional: colorful craft beads

Preparation: Make a copy of the necklace pieces and HomeLink for each child. You may wish to cut out the necklace pieces for younger children. Cut out cardboard backing or craft fun foam for each necklace piece. Cut a two-foot length of yarn or lanyard cord for each child.

Directions: Have the children color the necklace pieces and cut them out. Help the children glue each necklace piece onto a backing piece. Punch a hole in the top of each backing piece. Let the children string their pieces onto the yarn. As an option, the children could string beads between the necklace pieces. Knot each child's yarn at the ends to create a necklace. Put the necklace and HomeLink in a resealable bag to send home.

HomeLink: John 4:46-54

In today's Bible story, Jesus healed the son of a king's officer. The officer's son was important to Jesus. Your child is too. This necklace will remind your child of that.

Feel free to review the Bible story with your child during the week: **A man who worked for the king had a son. The son was very sick. The man traveled to another town to ask Jesus to help his son. Jesus told the man to go home—his son would be well! On the way home, the man met his servants. They told him that his son was well. Jesus had helped the man!**

GCE3: Blind Sculptures

Supplies: Blindfold for each child · Play dough or craft clay · Optional: table cover · Copy of the HomeLink note for each child

Directions: Blindfold each child. Let the children form a clay sculpture of their choice while blindfolded. While they are blindfolded, remind them of the story of the man born blind. This tactile experience will help the children remember his experience with Jesus in a more personal way. Give the children an opportunity to talk about what they have made and how the experience was for them.

You may want to give the children simple ideas of what to make from clay, such as a cross, smiley face, heart, or a star.

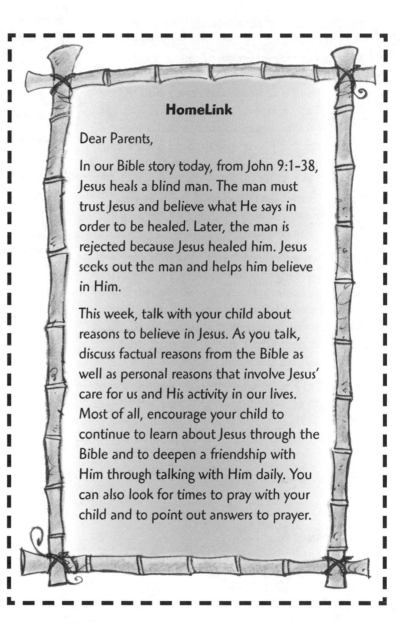

HomeLink

Dear Parents,

In our Bible story today, from John 9:1–38, Jesus heals a blind man. The man must trust Jesus and believe what He says in order to be healed. Later, the man is rejected because Jesus healed him. Jesus seeks out the man and helps him believe in Him.

This week, talk with your child about reasons to believe in Jesus. As you talk, discuss factual reasons from the Bible as well as personal reasons that involve Jesus' care for us and His activity in our lives. Most of all, encourage your child to continue to learn about Jesus through the Bible and to deepen a friendship with Him through talking with Him daily. You can also look for times to pray with your child and to point out answers to prayer.

GCP3: Invisible Picture

Supplies: White drawing paper · White crayons · Blue tempera paint · Water · Wide paintbrushes · Paint shirts · Old newspapers or table coverings · Copy of the HomeLink for each child

Preparation: Using a white crayon, draw a cross and the message "I can believe in Jesus" on white paper. Make one for each child. (You may need to go over each letter a couple of times to build up a waxy surface.) Make a copy of the HomeLink for each child. Add water to the tempera paint to make a thin paint.

Directions: This craft is a crayon resist. Because water doesn't absorb on top of wax, painting over the prepared paper causes a message to appear.

Have the children wear paint shirts and work at a table protected by newspaper. Tell the children that there's a picture on their papers that they can't see. **In our Bible story, the man was blind. He couldn't see. There is something on your paper that is hard to see. Jesus made the man see. When you paint over your paper, what do you see?**

Show the children how to brush the paint evenly over their entire piece of paper. When the picture and message appear, let the kids tell what the picture is. Read the message to them. Set the papers in a safe place to dry.

HomeLink: John 9:1-38; 20:31

Today's craft helped your child "see" a hidden message. Hang the message in a prominent place during the week. Be sure to talk about the message, "I can believe in Jesus."

You may also want to review the Bible story together. Let your child close his or her eyes while the man in the story is blind and then open them when Jesus heals the man.

There was a man who couldn't see. He was blind. One day Jesus and His helpers walked by the man. Jesus made mud and put it on the man's eyes. Jesus told the man to wash his eyes in a special pool. When the man washed off the mud, he could see! Jesus went and talked with the man later. The man believed that Jesus was God's Son.

GCE4: Unique Sheep

Supplies: Copy of the Unique Sheep for each child · Dry cereal in various shapes · Dry pasta in various shapes and colors · Old spices or seasonings in various colors and textures · Glue

Directions: Give each child a copy of the Unique Sheep and access to the supplies you gathered. Explain that the children may decorate their sheep in any way to make it unique—special and different. The children may glue on pasta, cereal, and spices in any pattern or shape to make their sheep special.

HomeLink

You are important to Jesus!
He is like a Good Shepherd, and you are like His sheep. You are unique—that's special and different from everyone else.
Jesus knows all about you.
And He loves you.

You are important to Jesus!

GCP4: Good Shepherd Banner

Supplies: Copy of the Good Shepherd picture for each child · Crayons or washable markers · Cotton balls · Glue · Felt squares · Scissors

Directions: Let the children color the picture of Jesus as the Good Shepherd. Have the children glue cotton balls on the sheep. Have the children cut out the picture on the solid black line. Let each child glue his or her picture to a felt square to create a banner. Glue the HomeLink to the back of the banner.

HomeLink: John 10:1-15

In today's Bible story Jesus told about the Good Shepherd and His sheep. Help your child hang the banner in a special place for the week. You may want to use the following simple story to talk about the banner with your child.

A shepherd watches over his sheep. He feeds the sheep. He keeps the sheep safe. The sheep are important to the shepherd.

Jesus is our Good Shepherd. We are important to Him. He loves us.

GCE5: Jesus Calms the Storm Picture

Supplies: Copies of "Jesus Calms the Storm" · Colored pencils · Green and blue tissue paper · Glue

Preparation: Make a copy of the "Jesus Calms the Storm" picture for each child.

Directions: The children will create pictures of Jesus calming the sea by using the picture below. Let the children color their pictures. Then show the children how to tear pieces of tissue paper to make the waves. The jagged edges will look like real waves. For rough water (before Jesus has commanded the calm), the tissue paper may be glued on with edges sticking up. For smooth waves (after Jesus has calmed them), the children may glue the tissue paper on flat. Let the children choose whichever part of the story they wish to depict.

HomeLink

Jesus helped His friends when they were scared. He calmed a bad storm! (Mark 4:35-41)

Jesus can also help you when you're scared or sad or upset. Just call on Him for help!

GCP5: Jesus and His Friends in the Boat

Supplies: Copies of Bible story figures · Scissors · Colored pencils or crayons · Brass paper fasteners

Preparation: Make a copy of the Bible story figures and HomeLink for each child. Cut out the figures and boat for the children.

Directions: Let the children color the figures of the boat, helpers, and Jesus. Help each child attach the figures of Jesus and the helpers to the boat by pushing a brass paper fastener through the X on the figure of the helpers and then through the X on the left side of the boat. Open the fastener in the back to secure the figures. Repeat for the Jesus figure on the right side of the boat. Show the children how to turn the Jesus figure to make it lie down or stand up. Send home a copy of the HomeLink with each child.

HomeLink: Mark 4:35-41

In today's Bible story, Jesus showed God's power by stilling a storm. Encourage your child to use today's craft as you retell the Bible story throughout the week. Pause after each sentence to let your child show the action of the story.

Jesus and His helpers took a boat out onto a lake. Jesus was tired. He fell asleep in the back of the boat. Suddenly the wind blew and the rain came down. Jesus' helpers were scared! They woke Jesus up. Jesus stood up and told the wind and rain to stop. Everything was calm. There was no more wind or rain. Jesus showed us what God is like by stopping the wind and rain. Jesus can do anything!

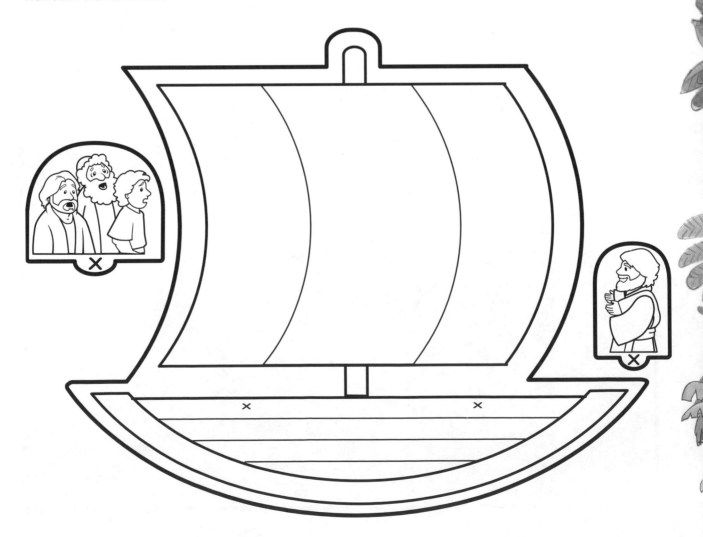

GCE6: Folding Bible Story Picture

Supplies: Copies of the Folding Bible Story Picture · Markers or crayons · Glue · Scissors

Preparation: Make one copy per child of the Folding Bible Story Picture below.

Directions: Hand out a copy of the picture to each child. Have the children color and then cut out the picture on the solid black lines. Demonstrate how to fold the paper in half so the pictures are on the outside. Then fold each side toward the center fold so that the picture is hidden. (See the illustration.)

Next, glue the two center sections together so that each picture can be seen one at a time. Open the page so that half of the picture shows the paralyzed man and the other half shows the man standing next to Jesus. Finally, glue the HomeLink to the back of the picture.

HomeLink

Jesus healed the paralyzed man (John 5:1-15). When Jesus heals, He shows us God's power. Use this picture to tell the Bible story to your parents. Pray together for someone who is sick. And remember to praise God every day that He is powerful!

GCP6: Footprint Portraits

Supplies: Copies of the footprints and HomeLink · Crayons or washable markers · Scissors

Preparation: Make a copy of the footprints, two for each child, and the HomeLink, one for each child. If you have young children, cut out the footprints for them.

Directions: Each child will need two footprints. Use the patterns below, or have the children trace their own feet. The children will turn the footprints into Foot Portraits that look like people, with the heel being the head and the toes being the hem of the robe. One Foot Portrait should be colored to look like Jesus. The other should be colored to look like the man who couldn't walk. Help the children write "Jesus" and "Man" on the appropriate Foot Portraits. Let older children cut out their own Foot Portraits.

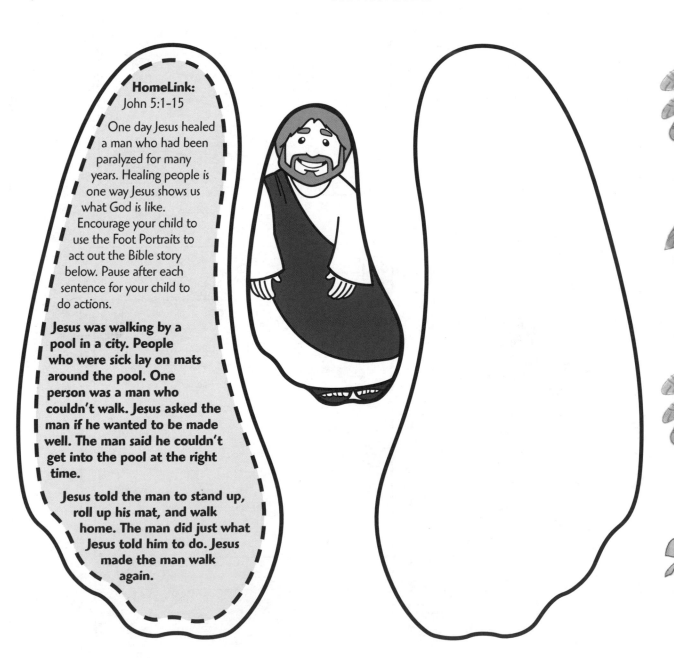

HomeLink:
John 5:1-15

One day Jesus healed a man who had been paralyzed for many years. Healing people is one way Jesus shows us what God is like. Encourage your child to use the Foot Portraits to act out the Bible story below. Pause after each sentence for your child to do actions.

Jesus was walking by a pool in a city. People who were sick lay on mats around the pool. One person was a man who couldn't walk. Jesus asked the man if he wanted to be made well. The man said he couldn't get into the pool at the right time.

Jesus told the man to stand up, roll up his mat, and walk home. The man did just what Jesus told him to do. Jesus made the man walk again.

GCE7: Following in Jesus' Footsteps

Supplies: Copies of the HomeLink paragraph · Construction paper of different skin colors · Pencils · Scissors · Strip of terry cloth fabric shaped like a small towel for each child · Craft or fabric glue or a stapler and staples

Preparation: Make a copy of the HomeLink paragraph for each child.

Directions: Have the children remove a shoe and sock and trace around one of their feet with a pencil on construction paper. They may draw the details of their foot (toe lines, toenails, freckles) and cut out the shape. On the back, the children glue a copy of the HomeLink paragraph. They may need to cut around it to fit the shape of their foot. Have the children glue or staple the strip of terry cloth towel across the front of the foot to represent the Bible story of Jesus washing his helpers' feet.

HomeLink

When Jesus washed His helpers' feet, He was showing them God's love (John 13:1-17, 34-35).

Jesus wants us to show His love to others.
Be like Jesus: Serve and love others!

GCP7: Foot Washing Puzzle

Supplies: Copies of the puzzle and HomeLink · Crayons · Scissors · Resealable plastic bags

Preparation: Make a copy of the puzzle and HomeLink for each child.

Directions: Let the children color the picture of Jesus washing the feet of His friends. As they color, talk about what is happening in the picture. Help the children cut their puzzles on the dashed lines. Have the children put their puzzle pieces in a resealable plastic bag with the HomeLink.

HomeLink: John 13:1-17, 34-35

Jesus shows us what God is like. In today's Bible story, Jesus showed God's love through serving His friends. He washed their dusty feet. Help your child put the Bible story puzzle together. Then help your child retell the story with these questions:

Jesus and His friends were having a big dinner. Point to Jesus and His friends. **Where are the dirty feet? Where is a towel? Where is a bowl? Who is washing feet? Can you find the puzzle piece that is shaped like a heart? Hearts remind us of love. Jesus shows us what God is like by serving His friends. He is showing love to them.**

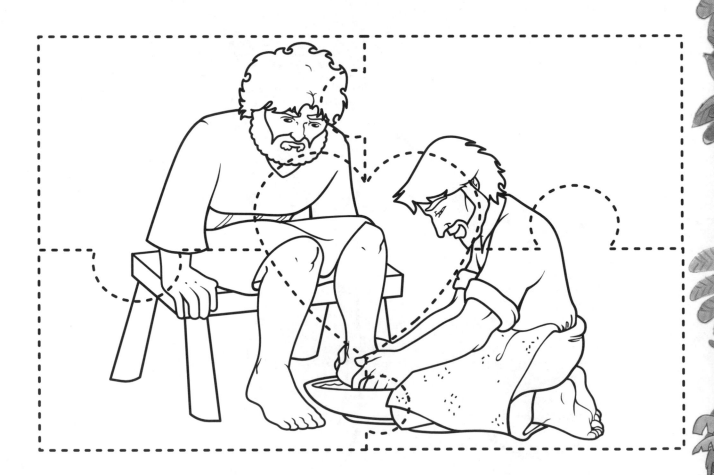

GCE8: The Forgiven Son

Supplies: Copies of the Forgiven Son picture · Markers · Glitter glue · Ribbon, rickrack, or fabric scraps · Fabric glue · Scissors · Optional: metallic crayons

Directions: Give each child a copy of the Forgiven Son picture. Ask the class if they know who it is *(the son from the Bible story after he has been forgiven by his father)*. Let the children decorate the necklace with glitter glue, and the robe with fabric scraps, ribbon, or rickrack. (Instead of fabric, the picture could be colored with metallic crayons.) They may color the rest of the picture.

HomeLink

Jesus told a story about a son who did what was wrong. Later the son felt bad and came back to tell his father he was sorry. The father forgave the son and loved him (Luke 15:11-24). Through this story Jesus showed us that God is like that father. He loves us and forgives us. This week ask for forgiveness if you do wrong and be willing to forgive others.

GCP8: Forgiven Son Puppets

Supplies: Copies of the finger puppets and HomeLink · Colored pencils · Clear tape · Resealable plastic bags · Scissors

Preparation: Make a copy of the Forgiven Son Finger Puppets and HomeLink for each child. Cut out the finger puppets.

Directions: Give each child a set of six puppets, and let the children color the front and back of each puppet. Help the children tape the edges of each puppet to fit their fingers. Put each child's puppets and a copy of the HomeLink in a resealable plastic bag to take home.

HomeLink: Luke 15:11-24

Jesus' story of the prodigal son teaches us that God's love is like the love of a forgiving father. Have your child use the finger puppets as you read the following story.

Here is a father. Here is a son. The father gave the son some money. The son took the money and moved far away. The son spent his money doing wrong things. Soon the son didn't have any money. He needed to eat. He needed new clothes. The son found a job feeding pigs. The pigs had food. The son still didn't have food. He decided to go home.

The father saw his son coming home. The father ran to his son and gave him a hug. The son told the father he was sorry for all the wrong things he had done. The father forgave the son. Jesus tells us what God is like. God is like the father. He loves us.

GCE9: Acts of Kindness Jellybean Jar

Supplies: Copies of jellybeans and HomeLink · Small jars with lids or paper cups with lids · Colored markers · Scissors · Glue · Optional: clear self-adhesive paper · Optional: jellybean stickers or colored sticker circles · Optional: jellybeans

Preparation: Make a copy of the jellybeans and the HomeLink for each child. If you are using clear, self-adhesive paper, cut strips the size of the jars or cups.

Directions: Have the children color the jellybeans with colored markers. Have the children cut out the jellybeans and glue them to a jar or cup. You may want to put a strip of clear contact paper around the jar or cup to secure the jellybeans. An alternative is to use stickers of jellybeans or brightly colored sticker circles to represent jellybeans. Give each child a copy of the HomeLink to roll up and put inside their jar to take home. You may also put one or two jellybeans in each child's jar.

HomeLink

Your child learned today how important it is to Jesus that we are kind to others. He will not forget all the kind things we have done. It's like we are being kind to Him! (Matthew 25:31-40)

Use this jellybean jar to help your child be aware of kind things he or she does. This week, whenever you see your child being kind, add a jellybean, penny, or other treat to this jar. Thanks for encouraging your child to be kind!

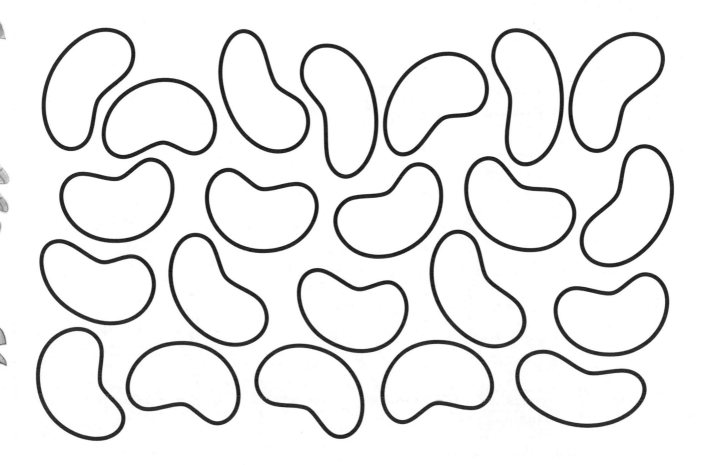

GCP9: A House Built on a Rock

Supplies: Copies of the house and HomeLink for each child · Crayons · Scissors · White craft glue · Rock for each child

Preparation: Collect a rock for each child in your class. Each rock needs to be big enough to glue the house from this page on it. Scrub off any dirt on the rocks. Make a copy of the house and the HomeLink for each child. If you have young children, cut out the houses for them.

Directions: Let the children color the houses, and help them cut them out. Help each child fold the tabs "inside" the house. Show the children how to glue the tabs to the rocks to "build" their houses on rocks. The children may need to hold the tabs onto the rock until the glue begins to set. While they are waiting for the glue to set, talk together about the builders in the story. When dry, place a copy of the HomeLink under each paperweight for the children to take home.

HomeLink: Luke 6:46-49

Today your child learned that Jesus shows us what God is like by telling special stories. The special story told in class was the parable of the two builders. The following story can be told throughout the week. Use the paperweight to help tell the story.

Jesus told special stories to show us what God is like. One day He told a story about two builders. One man built his house on a big, strong rock. Have your child point to the rock, then the house. **A big storm came. What happened to the house on the rock?** *(It kept standing.)*

Another man built his house on sand. The big storm came to his house too. What happened to the house on the sand? *(It fell down.)*

Jesus said that the people who hear God's Word and do what it says are like the man who built his house on the rock. Jesus told this story to help us understand what God is like.

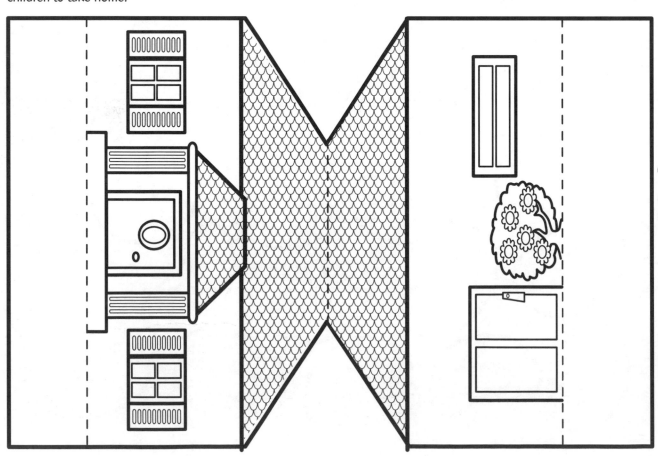

GCE10: Light in Darkness Picture

Supplies: Copies of the HomeLink paragraph · Black, yellow, white construction paper · Scissors · Glue · Star stickers · Optional: tempera paints and brushes

Preparation: Make a copy of the HomeLink paragraph for each child.

Directions: Give each child a piece of black construction paper, and have them fold it in half. Have them use the left side to show the creation of light and the right side to show the creation of the sun, moon, and stars. For the light, let the children cut or tear strips of white or yellow paper. They glue these on the left side as streams of light breaking up the darkness. For the right side, have the children cut or tear a sun and a moon from yellow paper and glue them down. Give out star stickers to put with the sun and moon.

Have the children glue a copy of the HomeLink paragraph to the back of their Light in Darkness Pictures.

If you prefer, you may let the children paint with white and yellow tempera paint rather than cut and glue with paper. For this option, splash white paint on the left side of the paper by lightly flicking a brush or by lightly squeezing a sponge. On the right side, the children may use yellow paint to make stars, sun, and moon with a brush or sponge shapes.

HomeLink

Totally dark! Then totally light! God did an amazing thing when He made light (Genesis 1:1-5, 14-19). What do you like about the dark? What do you like about light? Talk it over with your parents. Then pray with them to thank God for creating light.

GCP10: Creation Story Accordian Book

Supplies: Copies of the Creation book pattern and HomeLink · Construction paper · Crayons · Glue sticks · Optional: glow-in-the-dark star stickers

Preparation: Make a copy of the Creation Accordion Book and HomeLink for each child. Cut out the story strips. Accordion-fold the pages on the solid lines; then unfold them. Cut two pieces of construction paper, $3\frac{1}{2}$" by $4\frac{1}{2}$", for each child. On one piece write "God made . . ." These will be the covers for the books.

Directions: Give each child a copy of the story strips for a Creation Accordion Book. Have the children color the pictures. As an option, you may let the children put glow-in-the-dark stickers on the moon and stars page. Show the children how to put the book together. For the front cover, have each child glue the back of the day page to the back of a prepared cover. Have the children fold the pages back and forth on the fold lines and then glue the back of the moon and stars page to the other piece of construction paper. Let each child glue a HomeLink to the back cover of his or her book. Read the book together as a class.

HomeLink:
Genesis 1:1-5, 14-19

God made the world! This week's story taught how God made light—day, night, sun, moon, and stars. Review the Bible story throughout the week by reading this Creation Accordion Book with your child. As you read, point to each word on the page and let your child say it. Encourage your child to tell as much as possible about the day, night, sun, moon, and stars that God made.

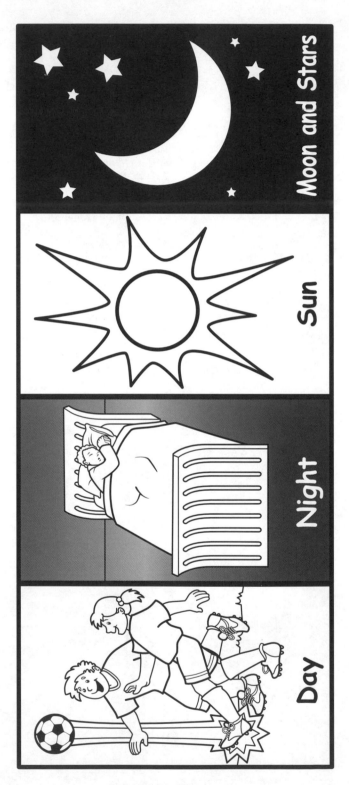

GCE11: Sky, Water, and Land Picture

Supplies: Copies of the HomeLink paragraph · Paper plates · Glue · Blue cellophane · Sandpaper · Blue colored pencils · Cotton balls · Scissors

Preparation: Make a copy of the HomeLink paragraph for each child.

Directions: Let the children each create a picture of the parts of creation learned about in today's Bible story. They may use a paper plate as the background, blue cellophane for water, sandpaper for land, blue pencil to color the sky, and cotton balls for clouds. (If paper plates are not available, the picture can be created in the box below.) Encourage creativity; there is no right or wrong way for them to depict creation. When finished, have each child glue a copy of the HomeLink paragraph to the back of their Sky, Water, and Land Pictures.

> **HomeLink**
>
> God created the sky, water, and land by His powerful hand. He made our world beautiful. He made our world useful. He made our world with everything we need. Praise God for His creation! (Genesis 1:1-10; Psalm 65:6-7; Amos 4:13)

GCP11: Creation Stained Glass Picture

Supplies: Copies of the picture and HomeLink · Colored pencils · Cotton balls · Baby oil · Old newspapers · Optional: paint shirts · Hole punch · Yarn · Resealable bags

Preparation: Make a copy of the creation picture and HomeLink for each child.

Directions: Let the children use colored pencils to color their pictures.

When finished coloring, help the children create the stained glass look: Lay the pictures on newspaper. Put a small amount of baby oil on a cotton ball for each child. The children rub the cotton ball across their picture to create a translucent look. Add more oil to the cotton balls as needed. The children will need to wash their hands with soap when finished.

Punch a hole in the top of the Stained Glass Picture and the HomeLink. Tie a 10" piece of yarn through each hole. Put the two ovals in a resealable plastic bag to take home.

HomeLink:
Genesis 1:1-10; Psalm 65:6-7; 135:7; Amos 4:13
God created the sky, water, and land. Hang your child's creation picture in a window where the light can shine through it. During the week, use the following action story to review what God made.

God made the world.
(Point up.)
He made the day and the sun.
(Make a circle above your head with your arms.)
God made the night, moon, and stars too.
(Cover your eyes.)
God made the sky.
(Stretch arms up high.)
He made the oceans.
(Ripple your fingers.)
He made the land.
(Make a mountain with your hands.)
Everything God made was very good!
(Point up.)

GCE12: Seasons All Around Mobile

Supplies: Copies of the Seasons Poem · Scissors · Glue · Old newspapers · Paint shirts · Blue or white butcher paper, poster paper, or large construction paper · Green, brown, pink, yellow, and white tempera paint · Paintbrushes · Water to clean brushes · Yarn (four 12" pieces per child) · Tape · Hole punch

Preparation: Make a copy of the Seasons Poem for each child, and cut them out. Cut blue construction paper in 6" x 18" strips, one for each child. (You may need to tape together shorter strips.) Divide each paper into four equal segments, side by side, and draw a line with marker to separate them.

Directions: Protect the tabletops with newspaper and the children's clothing with paint shirts. Set up five painting stations with paint and brushes: tree station—brown paint; winter station—white paint; spring station—pink paint; summer station—green paint; fall station—yellow paint. Have a Park Patrol member at each station to supervise and help.

The children begin at the tree station and paint four tree trunks with a few simple branches, one in each section of their paper. Then they may go to the other stations in any

order to paint a season for each tree trunk. White is for winter snow, pink is for spring blossoms, green is for summer's leaves, and yellow is for fall's changing and falling leaves.

After the paint has dried, help the children tape the ends of each picture together to form a circle, with the trees on the outside. This shows that the seasons are continuous and flow from one to the other. Attach a length of yarn to each season, and draw them together to meet in the middle, so the mobile can be hung. Have each child glue a Seasons Poem on an unpainted spot on their mobile.

HomeLink

Thank You,
God, for all four seasons:

Summer,
winter,
spring,
and fall.

We can see Your mighty power

'Cause You're the one
who made them all.

(Genesis 1:14)

GCP12: Seasons Child and Cards

Supplies: Copies of the Seasons Child, Cards, and HomeLink · Washable markers · Scissors · Resealable plastic bags

Preparation: For each child, make a copy of the Seasons Child and set of four seasons cards. Cut out the child shapes. Cut out the face holes in each seasons card. (You may want to enlist the help of the Park Patrol to cut out these pieces in advance.)

Directions: Have each child color a child figure and four seasons cards. Help the children cut apart the seasons cards on the dark lines. Show the children how to place the seasons cards over the child figure to change the seasons. Pack a set of cards, a child figure, and the HomeLink in a resealable plastic bag for each child.

HomeLink: Genesis 1:14; Psalm 147:15-18; Song of Songs 2:11-13a

God made the four seasons! Let your child use the figure and seasons cards to act out the following Bible story. You may want to mix up the seasons once your child learns them.

Here is our friend. God made a season where it rains. The flowers grow new leaves and blossoms. Can you dress our friend for spring? Put on the spring card.

It is hot. The trees have green leaves. How would our friend dress for summer? Put on the summer card.

God has changed summer to fall. The leaves are falling off the trees. What would our friend wear in the fall? Put on the fall card.

God sends snow to some places in winter. The weather is cold. Can you dress our friend for the cold winter? Put on the winter card.

GCE13: Animal Mosaic

Supplies: Copies of the HomeLink paragraph · Construction paper · Small bits of fabric scraps of different textures and designs · Glue

Preparation: Make a sample of the craft to show the children what a mosaic is. Make a copy of the HomeLink paragraph for each child.

Directions: Give each child a piece of construction paper. Place the fabric scraps where all can reach them. Explain to the children how to make a mosaic out of fabric scraps. The children choose scraps and arrange them on the paper to look like an animal, bird, or fish. Once arranged, the children pick up one scrap at a time and put glue under it to hold it to the paper. Encourage the children to remove only one scrap at a time or they will have a hard time re-creating their animal. Give each child a HomeLink paragraph to glue on the back of their animal, bird, or fish.

HomeLink

God is powerful. God is creative. Just look at all the animals He made! Birds, bugs, fish, sea critters, wild animals, farm animals, pets—God made them all. Every time you see an animal this week, stop and thank God for creating it.

GCP13: Animal Picture

Supplies: Copies of the animal pictures and HomeLink · Crayons · Scissors · Construction paper · Glue sticks

Preparation: Make a copy of the animal pictures and HomeLink for each child.

Directions: Let the children color the pictures of the animals. It is fine if the children color the animals a unique color. Help the children cut out the animals. Then the children may glue their animals on construction paper to make their own picture. Glue the HomeLink to the back of each child's picture.

HomeLink: Genesis 1:20-25; Psalm 104

God created animals, birds, and fish! Encourage your child to enjoy God's creation of all sorts of animals by looking for them and naming them throughout the week. The following story gives your child a chance to name animals while reviewing the Bible story.

God made animals. What kind of animals live in the water? What animals fly in the sky? What animals live on a farm? Even little bugs are animals that God made. Can you tell me about a bug? What animals live in the wild? God made all those animals. God made a wonderful world!

GCE14: My Angel Planner

Supplies: White construction paper or card stock · Two white feathers for each child · Markers or colored pencils · Glue · Optional: scissors

Preparation: Make a copy of the Angel Planner and HomeLink for each child on white construction paper or cardstock.

Directions: First talk with the kids about any plans they may have for the coming week. The kids should write them on their planners. Then let the children color their Angel Planners and glue two white feathers on the wings. (Explain to the children that in the Bible, some angels are described with wings and others are not. Some angels are described as bright and shiny while others are disguised to fit in with ordinary people. For this craft, the angel is shiny with wings.) If you choose to cut out the planners, then glue the HomeLink to the back.

HomeLink

Do you have big plans for this week? Write your plans on this Angel Planner. Stop and talk over each of your plans with Jesus. Talk about your plans with your parents, too. Look at your Angel Planner every day to remind you that God cares about you and His plans for you.

GCP14: Stand-up Nativity Scene, Part One

Supplies: Crayons or washable markers · Scissors · Resealable plastic bags · Optional: glue, fabric scraps

Preparation: Make a copy of the stand-up Bible figures for each child and cut them out for younger children. Cut out the HomeLink from each sheet.

Directions: Let the children color the figures of Mary and the angel. Or have the children glue fabric scraps on the figures. If not already done, help the children cut out the figures on the solid lines. Show the children how to fold each figure on the dotted lines so that it can stand. Send home the figures and the HomeLink in a resealable plastic bag.

HomeLink: Luke 1:26-33

These Bible figures are Part One of a nativity set. Over the next four weeks, your child will be bringing home more stand-up figures to complete the set. The following skit will help your child review this week's Bible story.

The Bible tells us about Mary. Stand the Mary figure in front of you.

An angel visited Mary. Set the angel figure next to the Mary figure.

The angel told Mary that she would have a baby. The baby would be God's Son. His name would be Jesus.

Mary was happy to obey God's plan.

Mary

Angel

GCE15: Chalk Drawing

Supplies: Photocopy of picture below for each child · Colored art chalk · Hairspray · Pencils

Preparation: Make a copy of the picture below for each child in your class.

Directions: Before letting the kids color, talk over with them areas in their lives where they would like help in listening to or obeying God more closely. *(The kids may suggest things like getting along with siblings, doing their chores with a good attitude, or obeying parents and teachers.)* Have the children write at least one area on the back of their picture using pencil.

Then let the children use chalk to decorate their pictures to represent themselves sleeping on their pillow at home. Encourage them to color the pillow, pajamas, blanket, hair, and so on, to look like what is really theirs. The kids may combine two or three colors to make shades or detail. Remind the kids not to brush against the chalk with their arm while coloring.

When finished, have each child bring their picture to a well ventilated area and watch you lightly spray their picture with hairspray. This will seal the chalk so it doesn't rub off.

HomeLink

When Joseph went to sleep one night, he got a special message from God. Joseph learned that baby Jesus would be born. He learned that he should marry Mary. Joseph listened carefully. And then Joseph obeyed.

We all should listen carefully to God and obey Him. Listening and obeying help us grow in God. Hang up this picture to remind you to listen to God and obey Him.

GCP15: Stand-up Nativity Scene, Part Two

Supplies: Copy of Joseph figure and HomeLink for each child · Crayons or washable markers · Scissors · Resealable plastic bags · Optional: glue, fabric scraps

Preparation: Make a copy of the stand-up Bible figure of Joseph for each child. For younger children, you may want to cut them out ahead of time. Cut out the HomeLink from each sheet. If you have a child who was not in class last week, you should provide the Bible figures of Mary and the angel from Lesson 14 to do at home.

Directions: Let the children color the figure of Joseph. You could also let the children glue fabric scraps on him. If not already done, help the children cut out Joseph on the solid lines. Show the children how to fold on the dotted lines so that he can stand. Put each Joseph figure with a HomeLink into a resealable plastic bag.

HomeLink: Matthew 1:18-25

These Bible figures are Part Two of a nativity set, begun last week. During the first four weeks of this unit, your child will bring home more stand-up figures to complete the set. This skit will help your child review this week's Bible story.

The Bible tells us about Joseph. Stand up Joseph figure.

One night Joseph had a dream. Lay Joseph down.

An angel talked to him in his dream. Stand the angel next to Joseph.

The angel told Joseph that Mary would have a baby. The baby would be God's Son. His name would be Jesus. Remove angel and stand up Joseph.

Joseph listened carefully and obeyed God.

Joseph

GCE16: Paper Bag Stable

Supplies: Brown lunch bags · Newspaper · Tape · Small stickers Bible-time animals (cows, donkeys, camels, doves, etc.) · Tempera paints · Paintbrushes · Paint shirts · Dark marker · HomeLink for each child

Directions: Have the children crumple pieces of newspaper and stuff them into a paper lunch bag until it is mostly full. Show each child how to fold down the top about an inch or so and tape it shut. The folded flap will be the back.

Lay the bag on its side so the "stable" is wider than tall. On the back, have the children tape the HomeLink paragraph. On the front, have each child paint a stable roof at the top, adding sides and beams. They may also paint straw along the bottom.

Let the children place animal stickers in the stable. When the paint is dry, print the words "Welcome Jesus" across a top beam of the stable.

HomeLink

Jesus is born! Mary and Joseph welcomed baby Jesus into their family. The animals shared their stable with baby Jesus. The angels and shepherds celebrated baby Jesus.

We can welcome Jesus too! How can you welcome Jesus at home? Set your Paper Bag Stable where it will remind you to welcome Jesus.

GCP16: Stand-up Nativity Scene, Part Three

Supplies: Copy of this week's Bible figures (donkey and Jesus in manger) and HomeLink for each child · Crayons or washable markers · Scissors · Resealable plastic bags · Optional: glue, yarn, shredded yellow paper

Preparation: Make a copy of the stand-up Bible figure of the donkey and baby Jesus for each child. For younger children, you may want to cut them out ahead of time. Cut out the HomeLink from each sheet. If there are children who missed Lessons 14 or 15, provide them with copies of the figures for those lessons to do at home (pages GC·34 and GC·36 of this book).

Directions: Let the children color the figures of the donkey and Baby Jesus. As an option, children could glue yarn on the donkey's mane and tail and yellow paper scraps on the hay of the manger. If not already done, help the children cut out the figures on the solid lines. Show the children how to fold each figure on the dotted lines so that it can stand. Put the figures and HomeLink in a resealable plastic bag.

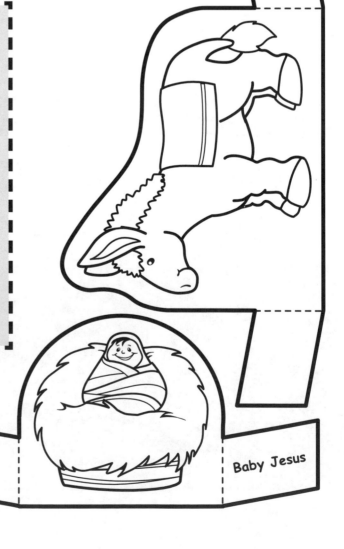

HomeLink: Luke 2:1-7

This week, the figures of a donkey and baby Jesus are added to your child's nativity set. Encourage your child to play with the figures while acting out the Bible story throughout the week. You could use the following skit with your child.

Mary and Joseph traveled to Bethlehem. "Walk" the figures of Mary, Joseph, and the donkey in front of you.

When they got there, the only place to stay was a stable. Have Joseph lead the donkey off to the side and come back to Mary.

It was time for baby Jesus to be born! Set the figure of baby Jesus in front of Mary and Joseph.

God sent His Son, Jesus.

GCE17: Picture the Nativity Posters

Supplies: Two or four standard-size sheets of poster board · Scissors · Craft glue · Various kinds of sticks (craft sticks, real twigs, toothpicks, small dowel rods, etc.) · Felt or fabric scraps · Any other craft supplies on hand (cotton balls, raffia, glitter, etc.) · Colored markers · Copy of "Picture the Nativity" Invitation for each child

Preparation: Depending on the wall space available in your classroom, plan to use either four full sheets of poster board, or cut two sheets of poster board in half to make four smaller pieces. Make copies of the "Picture the Nativity" Invitation on this page, one for each child.

Directions: Divide the children into four groups, and assign each group one of the Bible story scenes below.

Scene 1: Shepherds watching sheep at night in the fields

Scene 2: The angel of the Lord appearing to the shepherds

Scene 3: Huge group of angels singing in the night sky

Scene 4: Shepherds visiting baby Jesus, Mary, and Joseph in the stable

Tell the kids that they will create their assigned scene on poster board, and that the scenes will be hung up in order when dry. Help the groups brainstorm how they might depict their assigned scene using the craft supplies available. Also talk about how every person in the group can do part of the picture.

Rotate to each group to give help as necessary. When the scenes are finished, plan to hang them on a bulletin board or other wall space in your classroom or hallway. While the poster board pictures are drying, give out the "Picture the Nativity!" invitations and have the children fill in their scene number and the names of the others in their group.

YOU'RE INVITED!

The craft I worked on today is on display in my classroom. Please stop by and see it.

We made big posters of today's Bible story about the birth of Jesus. I worked on poster number _____.

The other kids who worked with me on this poster were:

_____

GOOD NEWS: JESUS IS BORN!

Love, _____

GCP17: Stand-up Nativity Scene, Part Four

Supplies: Copy of shepherds, sheep figures, and HomeLink for each child · Crayons or washable markers · Scissors · Resealable plastic bags · Optional: glue, fabric scraps, cotton batting

Preparation: Make a copy of the stand-up Bible figures of the shepherds and the sheep for each child. For younger children, you may want to cut them out ahead of time. Cut out the HomeLink from each sheet. If there are children who missed Lesson 14, 15, or 16, provide them with copies of the figures from those lessons to do at home.

Directions: Let the children color the figures of the sheep and shepherds. As an option, children could glue fabric scraps on the shepherds and cotton batting on the sheep. Show the children how to fold each figure on the dotted lines so that it can stand. Put the figures and HomeLink in a resealable plastic bag.

HomeLink: Luke 2:8-20

This week, the figures of shepherds and sheep were added to your child's nativity set to complete the collection. Encourage your child to play with the set throughout the week. Use the following skit to review the story.

Shepherds were taking care of sheep near Bethlehem. Set up the shepherd and the sheep.

An angel came to them. Hold the angel above the shepherds and sheep.

The angel said, "God's Son was born today in Bethlehem!" Set the angel aside.

The shepherds went to find baby Jesus. Set up Mary, Joseph, baby Jesus, and the donkey. Bring over the shepherds and sheep figures.

The shepherds found baby Jesus. The angels' good news was true!

GCE18: Worship Baton

Supplies: Unused paint sticks, dowel rods, or wrapping paper tubes · Colored markers · Crepe paper in two or three colors · Scissors · Clear tape · Glitter or metallic crayons · Glue · Copy of HomeLink paragraph for each child · Optional: inexpensive spray perfume

Preparation: Make a copy of the HomeLink paragraph for each child to take home.

Directions: Give each child a paint stick, dowel rod, or cardboard tube (call it a baton), and let the children use markers to color it. They should leave the bottom three inches plain so that the color does not come off on their hands when they hold it. Let the children choose colors of crepe paper they like and cut four or five streamers, each one about two feet in length. Help the children

tape their streamers to their batons. Let the children dot glue on open spots on their batons and drop glitter on the glue dots. (The children may color with the metallic crayons instead of using glitter.) As an option, lightly spray each baton with perfume to remind the children of the sweet-smelling gifts the wise men brought Jesus.

Next, have a parade or worship time! Read to the children the HomeLink paragraph. Play the Unit 4 song, "Glory, Glory," from the *Noah's Park Children's Church CD* or favorite Christmas songs that the children know by heart. Let the children stand or walk and carefully wave their batons in worship as they sing. Pass out the HomeLink paragraphs for the children to take home with their batons.

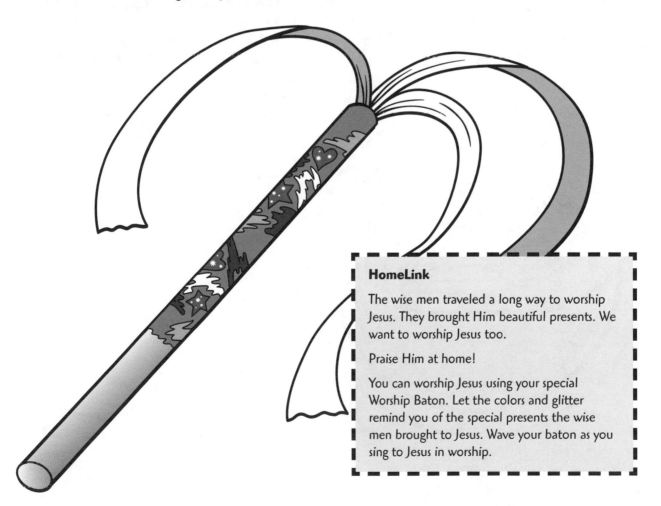

HomeLink

The wise men traveled a long way to worship Jesus. They brought Him beautiful presents. We want to worship Jesus too.

Praise Him at home!

You can worship Jesus using your special Worship Baton. Let the colors and glitter remind you of the special presents the wise men brought to Jesus. Wave your baton as you sing to Jesus in worship.

GCP18: Button Gift

Supplies: Small box or white lunch bag for each child · Copy of button pattern and HomeLink for each child · Crayons · Scissors · Stickers · A gift bow for each child · Optional: Clear self-adhesive paper

Preparation: Make a copy of the button pattern and the HomeLink for each child. If you have younger children, you may want to cut out the buttons for them ahead of time.

Directions: Let each child color a button and cut it out. As an option, you could cover each button (front and back) with clear self-adhesive paper to make it more durable. Also have each child decorate a small box or bag with stickers to look like a gift.

Have the children put their buttons inside their boxes or bags. Talk about how the wise men brought presents to Jesus. Tell the children that Jesus is like a wonderful present to us! Also put a HomeLink in each bag or box. Have the children attach bows to their gifts.

HomeLink: Matthew 2:1-11

In today's Bible story, the wise men visited Jesus. They brought gifts to worship Him. Your child made a craft to remember that God has given us a gift—His Son, Jesus. Let your child open and reopen the gift throughout the week. You could also tape a safety pin to the back of the button for your child to wear, or simply use masking tape to attach it to clothing.

You may use the following story to talk about the gift with your child.

Some wise men saw a star. They knew a king had been born. They packed presents for Him. They followed the star. The star led them to the new King. Who was the King? It was Jesus! The wise men gave Jesus their presents.

What's in your present? What does it remind you of? It's a button to remind you of a present for you from God. It's His Son, Jesus!

God gave me the gift of Jesus

GCE19: Today's News

Supplies: Copies of the newspaper, below · Pencils · Markers

Preparation: Make a copy of the newspaper below for each child.

Directions: Give each child a copy of the "Today's News" newspaper. Read the "news" together. Give out

pencils and markers, and show the children where to print their names. Help the children fill in the other information. Then encourage the children to draw a picture of themselves where indicated.

Today's News

God Knows All about _____ !
(your name)

We learned today that God made people.

One special person He made is _____.
(your name)

God knows all about this child. Here are some things God knows:

Birthday: _____.

Favorite food: _____.

Favorite toy: _____.

People in family: _____.

_____

_____

Other interesting things God knows about me:

_____

_____

_____

_____

Here is a picture of me doing my favorite thing.

GCP19: Adam and Eve Stained Glass Picture

Supplies: Copies of the Adam and Eve picture and HomeLink · Colored pencils · Old newspapers · Paint smocks · Vegetable oil · Small containers · Cotton balls · Resealable plastic bags

Preparation: Make a copy of the Adam and Eve picture and HomeLink for each child.

Directions: Have the children color their pictures using colored pencils. Then protect the tables with newspaper and the children with paint smocks. Show the children how to lightly dip a cotton ball in a small container of oil and rub the oil on their picture. This will create a translucent look to the picture, similar to stained glass. Be sure the children use just a small amount of oil on the pictures. When dry, place each picture and HomeLink in a resealable plastic bag.

HomeLink: Genesis 1:26-31; Psalm 139:1-18

God created people. He made us and knows all about us. Use this rhythmic version of the Bible story to help your child tell you what God made.

Tell me, tell me, who did God make? He made a man named Adam. Have your child point to Adam.

Tell me, tell me, who did God make? He made a woman named Eve. Have your child point to Eve.

Tell me, tell me, who did God make? He made you and me. Give your child a hug.

Tell me, tell me, what does God know? He knows where we go, what we do, what we think. Point up.

GCE20: My Working Gloves

Supplies: Adult size work gloves · White construction paper · Markers or crayons · Scissors · Hole punch · Yarn · Copy of HomeLink for each child · Glue or tape

Directions: Brainstorm with the kids some jobs that God gives them at home and school. Write these jobs on the board.

Have the children take turns trying on one of the work gloves and then tracing around it on construction paper. Then the children each choose five jobs they will do at home. They write one job on each of the five fingers of their paper glove. The children may decorate and cut out their paper work gloves. Punch a hole at the opening end of the glove and string yarn for hanging. Tape or glue the HomeLink to the back.

HomeLink

Talk with your parents about the jobs you help with at home. Decide on a place to hang your work glove as a reminder of the jobs God gives. You may find other jobs you can do and add them to your work glove if you wish.

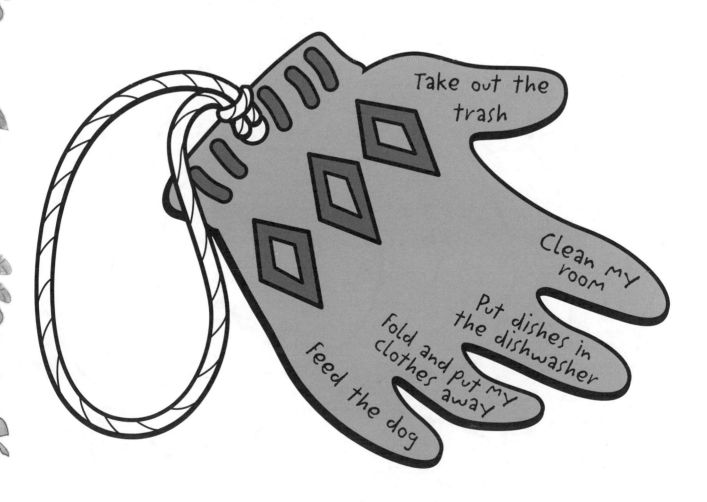

GCP20: Self-Portrait

Supplies: Copies of the body parts and HomeLink for each child · Construction paper · Fabric scraps · Yarn scraps · Glue · Crayons · Optional: hand mirror

Preparation: Make a copy of the HomeLink and a set of body parts for each child. Cut out the arms, legs, and faces before class. Cut fabric scraps into rectangles and triangles.

Directions: Give each child a piece of construction paper, two arms, two legs, and a head. Give all the children access to the fabric triangles and rectangles, yarn, and glue. Let the children use the pieces to put together a self-portrait. They use a fabric piece for their body and add head, legs, and arms. They may use yarn for hair and color their faces to look like their own. You may want to provide a mirror for the children to check the color of their eyes, hair, and so on. Help each child title his or her self-portrait "God Made My Body." Glue the HomeLink to the back of the picture.

HomeLink: Genesis 1:27; 2:7; 3:20; 4:1-2, 20-22; Psalm 139:1-6, 13-18

God made people. He made every part of our bodies. Use the following story throughout the week to review the Bible story with your child.

God made Adam and Eve. He made Cain and Abel. God made each with a head, arms, hands, legs, and feet. God made their bodies.

God made you too! Show me what parts of your body God made. God made your head. God made your arms. God made your legs. God made your feet. God made your body.

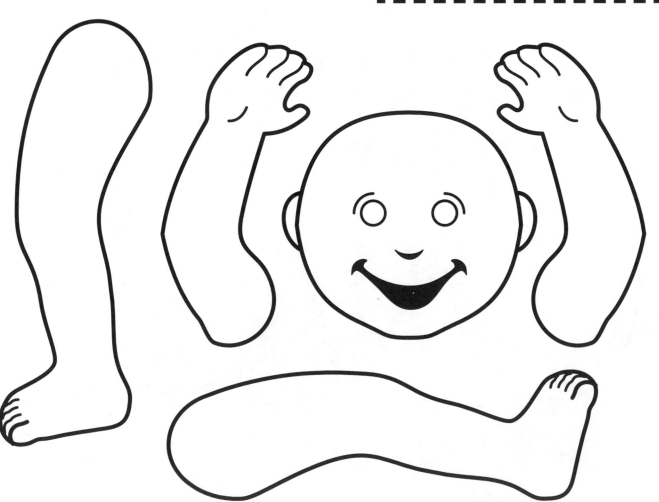

GCE21: Bible Story Puppets

Supplies: Copies of the HomeLink paragraph · Large-size craft sticks, two per child · Colored markers · Felt in red, brown, and other clothing colors · Yarn scraps in red, brown, and other hair colors · Scissors · Glue

Preparation: Make a copy of the HomeLink paragraph for each child. Make a sample of the Bible Story Puppet for the children to follow. Cut pieces of red and brown felt to fit the craft sticks, about 1" x 2".

Directions: With one craft stick, the children will make a back-to-back puppet of Esau and Jacob. With their second craft stick, the children will make a puppet of themselves.

Begin by giving each child one craft stick. Ask the children to describe Jacob and Esau from the Bible story. Instruct the children to decorate one side of their craft stick to look like Esau: They draw a simple face with marker, glue on a piece of red felt for clothing, and glue on a little red yarn for hair. Then have the children turn over their puppets. They decorate this side to look like Jacob: They draw a simple face with marker, glue on a brown piece of felt for clothing, and glue on a little brown yarn for hair. The children hold the bottom of the stick as a handle and may turn the puppet forward or backward to see Esau or Jacob.

Then give the children a second craft stick, and instruct them to decorate this to look like themselves. Let them choose what color yarn to glue on for hair and what color felt to use as clothing.

Have the children use pencil to write their names on the handle part of both puppets. When the children set their puppets aside, give each a HomeLink paragraph to place with their puppet and take home at the end of class.

HomeLink

You are specially made by God. He chose how you look. He planned what you're good at and like to do. He made all kids a little bit different from each other. The best part is that you are made by God. And you are special!

Play with your Bible story puppets this week to remind you that you are specially made by God! (Genesis 25:20-28)

GCP21: Esau and Jacob Puppets

Supplies: Copies of the puppet patterns and HomeLink · Colored pencils · Scissors · Tape · Craft sticks (two per child) · Resealable plastic bags

Preparation: Make a copy of the Esau and Jacob puppets and their add-on pieces for each child, and cut them out. Also copy the HomeLink for each child.

Directions: Have the children color the puppets of Jacob and Esau as well as the bow and arrow and bucket. (Esau should be a reddish color.) If you have older preschoolers you could let them cut out their own puppets.

Show the children how to tape a craft stick to the back of each puppet. Then lead the children in doing the HomeLink, using their puppets.

Put each child's puppets, the accessories, and a HomeLink in a resealable plastic bag to take home.

HomeLink: Genesis 25:20-28

God made each of us, but we are all different. Let your child use the stick puppets to act out the Bible story of Jacob and Esau throughout the week.

God made two boys. The oldest one was Esau. Have your child hold the Esau puppet in one hand. Esau was red. He had lots of hair. Esau liked to hunt. What did he use? Have your child put the bow and arrow on Esau.

The younger brother was Jacob. He had smooth skin. Have your child hold the Jacob puppet. He stayed near the tent and cooked. Have your child put the bucket on Jacob.

GCE22: Surprise Flap Picture

Supplies: Copies of the Bible story pictures and HomeLink · Markers or crayons · Construction paper · Scissors · Glue · Tape

Preparation: Make copies of the Bible story pictures, one set of six for each child. Cut construction paper squares (to serve as flaps) a little larger than each picture square, approximately 3 1/2" x 2 1/2". Cut six flaps for each child.

Directions: Give each child a set of Bible story pictures to color. When finished, have the children cut apart their pictures on the solid lines. Give each child a sheet of 9" x 12" construction paper and help them glue their six pictures down in order, with space between them. Then place a paper flap over each picture and tape it along the top. Each flap may be lifted to reveal the picture underneath. Number the flaps 1–6. Help them title their paper "How Did Jacob and Esau Get Along?" Glue the HomeLink to the back of the construction paper.

HomeLink

At home read these sentences with your parents to review today's Bible story.

1. Jacob and Esau were brothers. They were very different.

2. Jacob and Esau both wanted their father's blessing. Their father wanted to bless Esau.

3. Jacob played a mean trick on Esau. Jacob dressed up like his brother and got the blessing.

4. Esau was mad! Jacob moved far away so Esau wouldn't hurt him.

5. Jacob sent Esau a present and a message. Jacob was sorry for his mean trick.

6. Esau forgave Jacob. Esau went and gave his brother a hug.

GCP22: God Made Me Mirror

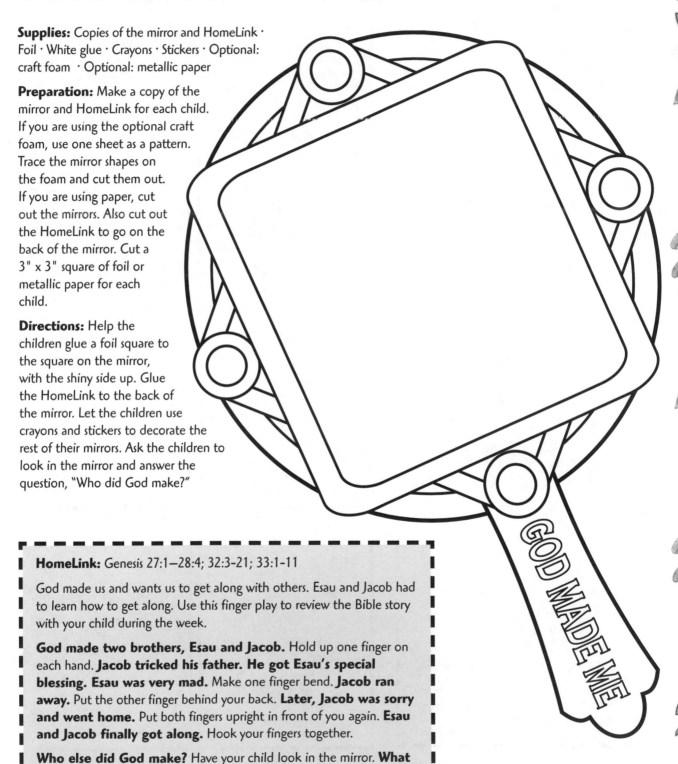

Supplies: Copies of the mirror and HomeLink ·
Foil · White glue · Crayons · Stickers · Optional:
craft foam · Optional: metallic paper

Preparation: Make a copy of the
mirror and HomeLink for each child.
If you are using the optional craft
foam, use one sheet as a pattern.
Trace the mirror shapes on
the foam and cut them out.
If you are using paper, cut
out the mirrors. Also cut out
the HomeLink to go on the
back of the mirror. Cut a
3" x 3" square of foil or
metallic paper for each
child.

Directions: Help the
children glue a foil square to
the square on the mirror,
with the shiny side up. Glue
the HomeLink to the back of
the mirror. Let the children use
crayons and stickers to decorate the
rest of their mirrors. Ask the children to
look in the mirror and answer the
question, "Who did God make?"

HomeLink: Genesis 27:1—28:4; 32:3-21; 33:1-11

God made us and wants us to get along with others. Esau and Jacob had
to learn how to get along. Use this finger play to review the Bible story
with your child during the week.

God made two brothers, Esau and Jacob. Hold up one finger on
each hand. **Jacob tricked his father. He got Esau's special
blessing. Esau was very mad.** Make one finger bend. **Jacob ran
away.** Put the other finger behind your back. **Later, Jacob was sorry
and went home.** Put both fingers upright in front of you again. **Esau
and Jacob finally got along.** Hook your fingers together.

Who else did God make? Have your child look in the mirror. **What
does God want you to do?** *(Get along with others.)*

GCE23: Joyful Giving Banks

Supplies: Copies of the coin pictures and HomeLink · Small box with a lid for each child · Colored markers · Scissors · Glue · Craft supplies (glitter glue; rickrack, sequins, or buttons, etc.) · Optional: paper lunch bags

Preparation: Make a copy of the coin pictures and HomeLink for each child. If you can't find a small box for every child, you may use paper lunch bags.

Directions: Give each child a set of coin pictures to color and cut out. Let each child glue their coins to a box. With whatever craft supplies you have on hand, let the children further decorate their boxes to turn them into Joyful Giving Banks.

As the children work, talk about the many different things that kids can give to God, using the pictures on the coins as clues. Put the HomeLink inside the box to take home.

HomeLink

You can give lots of things to God. Talk with your parents to think of some of the things you can give Him. Give with a big smile! (2 Chronicles 24:1–14)

GCP23: Offering Envelope

Supplies: Copies of the Offering Envelope and HomeLink · Crayons · Clear tape

Preparation: Make a copy of the Offering Envelope and HomeLink for each child. Cut out the envelopes and HomeLinks. Fold the envelopes on the dotted lines, and then unfold them.

Directions: Give each child an Offering Envelope. Read the words together, and let the children color the picture of Joash and the people giving their offerings. Show the children how to fold the envelopes and tape the sides together. Encourage the children to use their envelope to bring an offering to church. Give each child a HomeLink to place inside their envelope to take home.

HomeLink: 2 Chronicles 24:1-14

King Joash and the people brought their offerings to God so the temple could be repaired. The following story can help you review the Bible story with your child during the week. You will need a box and several coins to tell the story. Your child may want to bring the envelope back to church with an offering.

King Joash loved God. Have your child put a coin in the box. **He wanted to fix up the temple so people could worship God.** Have your child put a coin in the box. **King Joash and the people put offerings in a box.** Have your child put a coin in the box. **The offerings were used to fix the temple.** Have your child put a coin in the box. **King Joash and the people were able to worship God together in the temple.**

GCE24: Craft Stick Scroll

Supplies: Copies of the scroll (one per child) and HomeLink · Pieces of white or tan cloth or felt · Craft sticks (about 6" long) or pencils · Colored pencils · Craft glue · Optional: Bibles · Yarn

Preparation: Cut cloth or felt into rectangles about 8 3/4" x 4 3/4". Cut yarn into one-foot lengths (one per child).

Directions: Explain that books in Bible times were written on scrolls that were made of either thin leather or a different kind of paper than ours.

Give each child a copy of the scroll and colored pencils. Help the children think of a Bible verse they could write on their scroll. They might use the memory verse, or you could suggest other familiar verses, such as Psalm 23:1; John 3:16; or 2 Thessalonians 5:17. You may write these verses on the board for the children to copy or have the children look them up in a Bible.

Help the children glue their paper scrolls centered on a strip of cloth or felt. Then the children glue a craft stick or pencil on each narrow end of the cloth. Do not let the children roll up their scrolls until the glue is dry. Roll each side inward to meet in the center. Use a piece of yarn to tie it. Give out the HomeLink paragraph for the children to take home.

HomeLink

Retell the Bible story to your family. Then read the Bible verse you have written on your scroll. Talk about how we worship God by learning His Word. Consider making a plan with your family to help you learn more of God's Word.

My Bible Scroll

We worship God by learning His Word. ~Nehemiah 8:1-6

GCP24: Bible Scroll

Supplies: Copies of the Praise God word sheet · Clear tape · Crayons · Two ¹/₂" diameter dowel rods or sticks (cut to 5" lengths), or two pencils per child · Yarn

Preparation: Make a copy of the word sheet for each child. Cut them apart. Cut yarn into one-foot lengths.

Directions: Give each child a copy of the word sheet, and read it to them. Let the children color the words. Help the children tape each end of the paper to a stick. Show the children how to roll up the paper like a scroll and tie it with a piece of yarn.

HomeLink: Nehemiah 8:1-6

Ezra read God's Word to the people. They listened carefully and worshiped God. Encourage your child to act the part of Ezra reading from a scroll. Use this story to help your child.

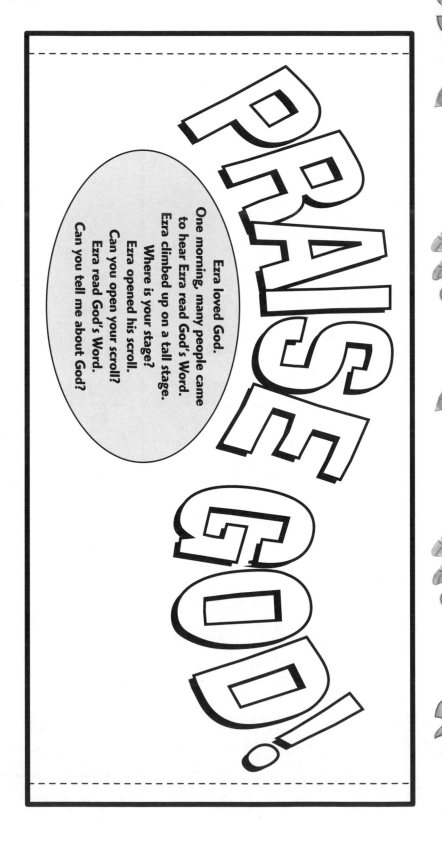

Ezra loved God.
One morning, many people came to hear Ezra read God's Word.
Ezra climbed up on a tall stage.
Where is your stage?
Ezra opened his scroll.
Can you open your scroll?
Ezra read God's Word.
Can you tell me about God?

PRAISE GOD!

GCE25: Prayer Reminder Magnets

Supplies: Copies of the magnet pictures · Cardstock · Utility knife or adult scissors · Markers · Glue · Magnetic tape · Clear, self-adhesive paper · Scissors

Preparation: Make a copy of the oval shape (surrounding the pictures). Trace it onto cardstock (or photocopy the magnet pictures directly onto cardstock), one for each child. Use a utility knife or strong scissors to cut out the ovals. Trace slightly larger ovals onto clear, self-adhesive paper, and cut them out. Make copies of the magnet pictures; each child will need only one of the three. Cut a two-inch strip of magnetic tape for each child.

Directions: Show children the three picture choices, and let each child choose one to color. Have the children glue their colored picture onto a cardstock oval. Help the children remove the backing from a clear, self-adhesive oval and place it on top of their picture. Show the children how to carefully trim off the excess clear covering. Let each child remove the backing from a piece of magnetic tape and attach it to the back of their picture.

HomeLink

Talk with your parents about what you have learned about worshiping God by praying. Then decide where you can put your magnet as a reminder to worship God each day in prayer.

GCP25: Prayer Reminder Card

Supplies: Copies of the Prayer Reminder Card and HomeLink · Washable markers · Clear tape · Optional: cardstock · Resealable plastic bags · Scissors · Utility knife

Preparation: Make a copy of the Prayer Reminder Card and HomeLink for each child. You may want to use cardstock for sturdier cards. Use scissors to cut along the outer solid line. Use a utility knife to cut along the solid line above the praying hands (without cutting the center fold line). Fold on the dashed lines.

Directions: Give each child a Prayer Reminder Card to color. Then show the children how to fold the center line as well as the tabs. Help them tape the bottom tabs together so that the Prayer Reminder Cards stand alone. Talk with the children about where they can place their Prayer Reminder Cards at home. Have the children put their Prayer Reminder Card and the HomeLink into a resealable plastic bag to take home.

HomeLink: 1 Kings 8

King Solomon led the people of Israel in prayer when he dedicated the new temple. Use the following story to review the Bible story with your child. Try to find a special time to pray together.

Here is King Solomon. Place your hands over your head like a crown.

King Solomon built a temple. Place your fingers together to form a peak.

People could worship God at the temple. Point up.

Many people came to the temple. Pat your knees as if walking.

King Solomon and the people prayed. Fold your hands.

They worshiped God by praying together. Point up.

TAPE HERE

I CAN PRAY TO GOD!

TAPE HERE

GCE26: Shaker Drums

Supplies: Copies of the music "stickers" and HomeLink · Small, empty containers (milk carton, tissue box, jello box, containers from yogurt, margarine, cocoa, etc.), one for each child · Dry rice or beans · Clear packing tape · White construction paper or gift wrapping paper · Small clear tape · Markers · Scissors · Glue · Optional: Noah's Park CD and CD player

Preparation: Make a copy of the music "stickers" for each child. Thoroughly clean and dry the boxes or plastic containers.

Directions: Give each child a container and a handful of dry rice or beans to put in it. Use clear packing tape to firmly tape the opening shut. (If using tissue boxes that have a wide opening, place construction paper over the opening and firmly tape it in place.) This forms the basic shaker drum.

Then let the children decorate their drums: First have them completely cover their boxes in white construction paper or gift wrap and tape like a present. (Be sure the Park Patrol members are available to assist with this project.) Then give each child a set of music "stickers" to color and cut out. Have the children glue their stickers to their shaker drums. Glue on the HomeLink as well.

If time permits, play a lively praise song and let the children shake their drums in time with the music.

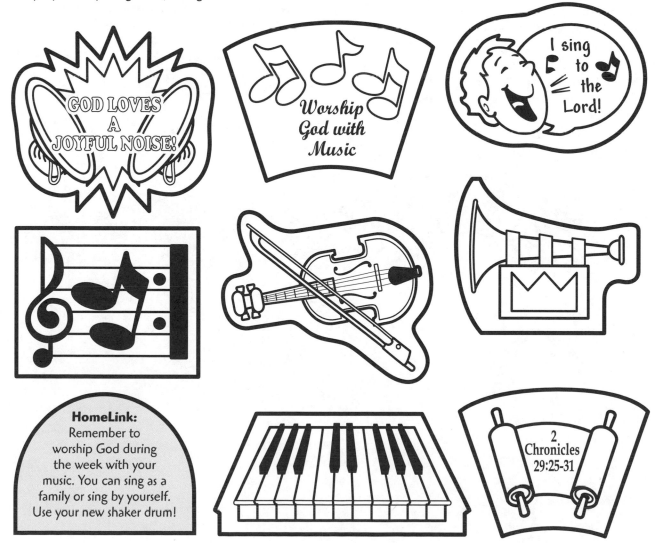

GCP26: Tambourines

Supplies: Copies of the "Praise God" circle and HomeLink · Small plastic or sturdy paper plate for each child · Hole punch · Two jingle bells for each child · Chenille wires · Crayons · Glue · Optional: Noah's Park CD and CD player

Preparation: Make a copy of the circles and HomeLink for each child. Cut them out. Punch two holes in the rim of each paper plate. Cut the chenille wires into six-inch lengths, two per child.

Directions: Give each child a "Praise God" circle to color. Help the children glue the circle to the bottom of a plate. Help them glue the HomeLink to the other side of the plate. Then show the children how to thread a chenille wire through the jingle bell and then through one of the holes in the plate. Help them twist the ends together. Repeat for the other hole. If time permits, play a praise song and let the children play along with their tambourines.

HomeLink:
2 Chronicles 29:25-31

King Hezekiah and the people of Jerusalem worshiped God with music. Look for ways you and your child can worship God with music this week. Let your child act out playing the different instruments as you read this story.

King Hezekiah loved God.
He wanted to worship God with music.
Many people came to the temple to worship God together.
The priests played trumpets: Toot-a-toot-toot!
Levites played cymbals: Crash, clang!
Others played harps: Plink-plonk!
The people sang
special songs.

GCE27: Power Mobile

Supplies: Copy of page for each child · Construction paper · Crayons or markers · Scissors · Glue · Yarn or chenille wire · Hole punch

Preparation: Make a copy of the page for each child.

Directions: Have the children first color and then cut out the "Jesus Is All-Powerful" sign. Then let each child pick out a color of construction paper and fold it in half. Have the kids glue the sign to one half of the construction paper. Cut around the sign. Then have each child cut a second "cloud shape." Use the hole punch and punch holes in the sign where indicated. Punch another hole in the second cloud shape. The children should tie a short piece of yarn to the top of the sign for a hanger. A longer piece of yarn (about 6" to 8") should be tied between the sign and the second cloud shape. On the second cloud the children can write ways that Jesus is all-powerful. Glue the HomeLink to the second cloud shape as well.

HomeLink: Jesus is all-powerful! Do you remember how Jesus raised Lazarus from the dead? Jesus can use that same power in YOUR life. Put this Power Mobile where you'll see it every day. Let it remind you that you can take all your problems to Jesus. Let His power help you!

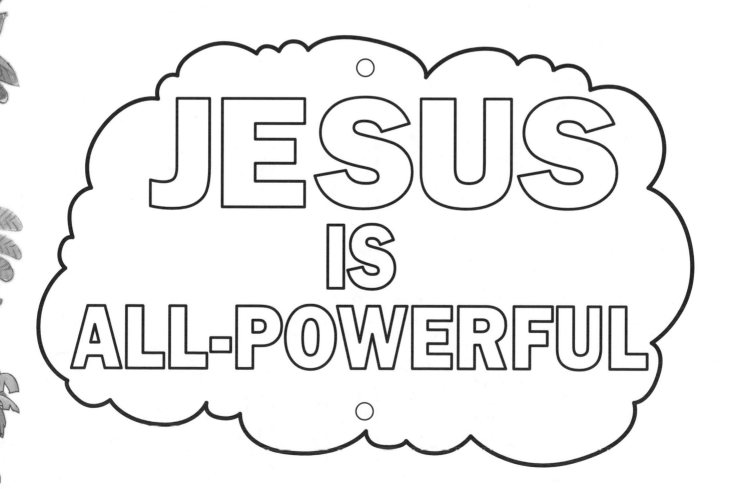

GCP27: Jesus' Love and Greatness Mobile

Supplies: Copy of mobile for each child · Crayons or colored pencils · Scissors · Yarn · Tape · Resealable plastic bags

Preparation: Make a copy of the mobile for each child, and cut out the HomeLink. You may want to cut out the mobile pieces before class if your students are too young to cut. Cut four six-inch-long pieces of yarn for each child.

Directions: Let the children color the mobile pieces. As they color, talk about what is on the pictures. If the pieces have not yet been cut out, help the children to do so now. Help each child tape an end of yarn to each piece at the Xs. Then help the children tape the other yarn ends to the mobile strip at the Xs. Tape one end of the fourth piece of yarn to the O on the strip to serve as a handle. Place the mobile and the HomeLink in a resealable plastic bag to send home.

HomeLink: John 11:1-45

Today your child heard how Jesus showed His love and greatness by raising His friend Lazarus from the dead. Encourage your child to point to each part of the mobile as you read the following story.

Jesus had three friends: Mary, Martha, and Lazarus. When Jesus was in another town, Lazarus became sick and died. Mary and Martha were sad. When Jesus came to see them, He was sad too. But Jesus knew something powerful was going to happen.

Jesus went with Mary and Martha to the cave where Lazarus was. He said, "Lazarus, come out!" And Lazarus walked out. He was alive!

GCE28: Doorknob Hanger

Supplies: Copies of the Doorknob Hanger and HomeLink paragraph on construction paper or cardstock · Crayons or markers · Scissors · Glue sticks · Glitter glue

Preparation: Make a copy of the "Jesus Can Help" Doorknob Hanger and the HomeLink paragraph for each child.

Directions: Have the children color their doorknob hangers and cut them out. They should each glue a HomeLink paragraph to the back. The children may further decorate the their doorknob hangers with glitter glue.

HomeLink

When the blind men asked Jesus for help, He helped them! Jesus shows His love and greatness by helping us, too.

Talk with your parents about ways Jesus might help you. Then pray together about anything you need help with.

Hang this on your doorknob to remind you to ask Jesus for help every day.

GCP28: Funny Glasses

Supplies: Copies of the glasses and HomeLink · Small stickers · Colored pencils · Clear tape · Colored acetate from report covers or colored plastic wrap · Optional: cardstock

Preparation: Make a copy of the glasses and the HomeLink for each child. For sturdier projects, copy them onto cardstock. Cut out the frames for each child. (A craft knife will help in cutting out the lenses.) Set aside the HomeLink to hand out at the end of class. For each child, cut two circles of acetate or plastic wrap a tiny bit larger than the lenses.

Directions: Let the children decorate their glasses with the stickers and colored pencils. Show the children how to tape the acetate or plastic wrap onto the frames for the lenses. Help each child tape the bows onto the frames. You may need to adjust the length of the bows to keep the glasses on the children's faces.

When finished, have the children put on their glasses and lead them in this discussion. **When you put on your glasses, it's hard to see things just the way they are. They may be a different color. Things may be blurry. It's harder to see. The men in our Bible story couldn't see. But Jesus made them see. Take off your glasses. Now you can see too.**

HomeLink: Matthew 20:29-34

What cool shades! But when you look through the glasses your child made, it's harder to see. That isn't anything like the problem two men had in our Bible story. They were blind. But when they asked Jesus for help, He made them see. Have your child put on his or her glasses as you talk about the Bible story throughout the week.

What can you see? The two blind men couldn't see anything. One day, they heard Jesus walking by. "Jesus, help us," they called. Jesus helped them. He made them see. Now take off your glasses. What can you see?

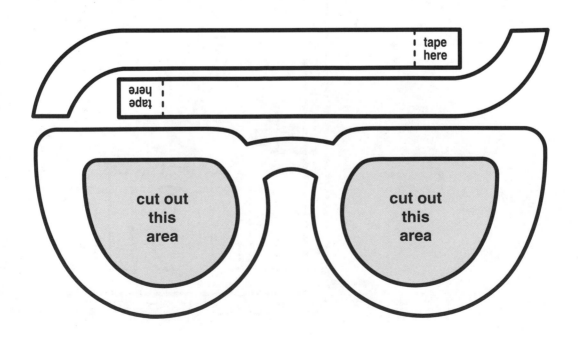

tape here

tape here

cut out this area

cut out this area

GCE29: Trust Jesus Poster

Supplies: Several copies of the Bible verses below · Copies of the HomeLink paragraph, one for each child · Chenille wire (or twist ties from garbage bags) · Scissors · Construction paper or poster board · Craft glue · Colored markers · Bible

Preparation: Make a copy of the Bible references and HomeLink paragraph for each child, and cut them out.

Directions: Show the children how to twist chenille wire (or twist ties) to form letters. (You may cut some shorter to make some letters easier.) After they practice, have each child spell the words "TRUST JESUS."

Give each child a sheet of construction paper or piece of poster board. Let the kids glue their "Trust Jesus" letters onto it. Give each child a HomeLink paragraph to glue onto the bottom of their posters. Then hand out the Bible verse papers. Look up and read the verses together. Instruct the children to each choose one verse that they think will remind them to trust Jesus during the week. Let each child cut out the reference he or she chose and add them to their posters. As time permits, the kids may write out the Bible verse on their posters.

HomeLink

Jesus' followers saw Him walk on water. Peter trusted Jesus and walked on water too. But when Peter became afraid, he stopped trusting and started sinking! Peter learned to keep on trusting Jesus, even when it was tough.

Jesus wants you to trust Him too. Hang this poster in a good spot at home. Talk with your parents about ways you can trust Jesus. Read together the Bible verses. Maybe you could even memorize them. Pray to Jesus every day. You'll see your trust in Him grow!

GCP29: Boat Magnet

Supplies: Copies of the craft pieces and HomeLink · Glue · Magnetic tape · Washable markers · Craft sticks · Scissors

Preparation: Make a copy of the craft pieces below and HomeLink for each child. Cut out the boat, sail, pocket piece, and people figures. Save the HomeLink to hand out at the end of class. Cut open the slit in each boat. Cut a two-inch piece of magnetic tape for each child.

Directions: Have the children color the boat, sail, and people figures. Help the children glue the boat and sail to the craft stick. Tape the pocket piece to the back of the boat on the side with the slit. This will keep the figures from falling out. Peel off the adhesive backing from the magnetic tape. Let each child put magnetic tape on the back of the boat. Show the children how to put the people figures into the boat.

HomeLink: Matthew 14:22-33

Jesus showed His love and greatness when He encouraged Peter to walk on the water with Him. Peter learned to trust Jesus. Your child can too. Use your refrigerator as the backdrop of the HomeLink this week. Let your child use the boat and figures to act out the story. While you tell each line, let your child choose how to portray the action:

Jesus' helpers went out in a boat.

Jesus came to see them, walking on the water.

Peter asked to come see Jesus.

Peter was afraid. He started to sink.

Jesus helped Peter get into the boat.

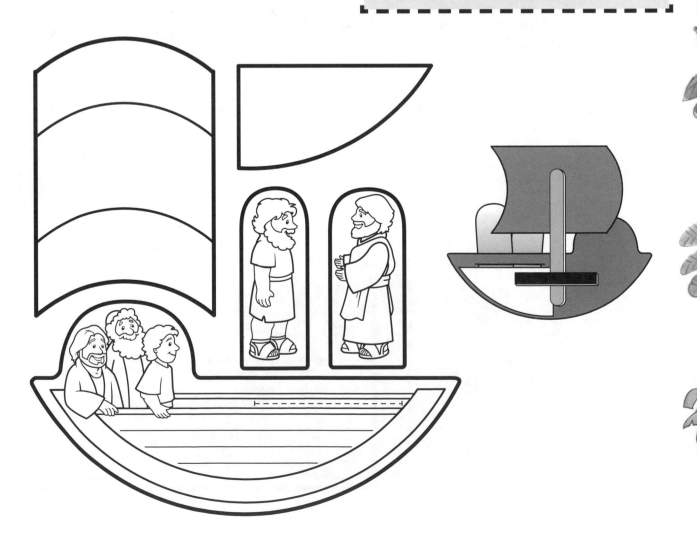

GCE30: Traveling with Jesus Board Game

Supplies: Copies of the Traveling with Jesus Board Game · Crayons or markers · Game markers (coins, buttons, little squares of paper, etc.) · Spinner or coins

Preparation: Make a copy of the Traveling with Jesus Board Game for each child.

Directions: Have the kids color the game board. They can pick one or two friends to play with, and choose one of their game boards to play on. Find something to use as game markers. Use a spinner, or flip a coin to decide how many spaces to move on each turn (heads—1, tails—2).

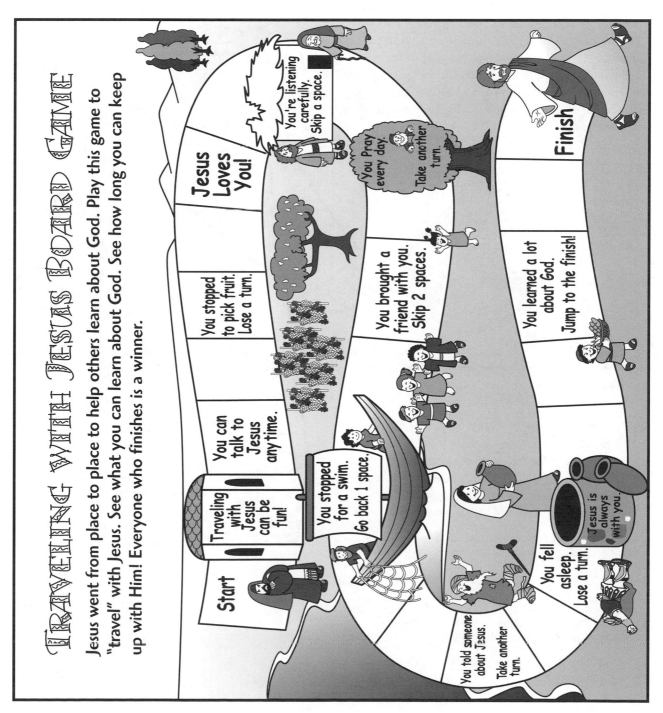

TRAVELING WITH JESUS BOARD GAME

Jesus went from place to place to help others learn about God. Play this game to "travel" with Jesus. See what you can learn about God. See how long you can keep up with Him! Everyone who finishes is a winner.

Start

Traveling with Jesus can be fun!

You can talk to Jesus anytime.

You stopped to pick fruit. Lose a turn.

Jesus Loves You!

You're listening carefully. Skip a space.

You Pray every day. Take another turn.

You stopped for a swim. Go back 1 space.

You brought a friend with you. Skip 2 spaces.

You learned a lot about God. Jump to the finish!

Finish

You told someone about Jesus. Take another turn.

You fell asleep. Lose a turn.

Jesus is always with you.

GCP30: Jesus Hand Puppet

Supplies: Copies of puppet pieces and HomeLink · Paper lunch bags · Washable markers · Scissors · Glue sticks

Preparation: Make a copy of the puppet pieces and HomeLink for each child. For younger children, cut out the puppet face and body.

Directions: Let the children color the face of Jesus and His body. Holding the bags upside down, help the children glue the face of Jesus on the folded part of the bag. Then help the children glue the body onto the side of the bag just under where the bottom is folded over. Have the children glue a copy of the HomeLink to the back of the puppet. The children work the puppets by putting their hands in the open end and curling their fingers into the folded part, moving their fingers up and down to make the puppet "talk."

HomeLink:
Mark 1:21-22, 29, 35-39; Luke 4:14-16

Jesus showed His love and greatness by teaching people about God. He traveled to synagogues and homes in many towns. Help your child retell the Bible story during the week using the Jesus Hand Puppet. You may use these questions to help your child tell the story.

Jesus and His helpers traveled. Where did they go? *(To many towns.)*

Jesus taught at a synagogue. What did He teach? *(About God.)*

Jesus taught at a house. What did He do? *(He made a sick woman well.)*

What does Jesus want us to do? *(Learn about God.)*

11-5-06

GCE31: Storytelling Seeds

Supplies: Copies of the Storytelling Seeds picture · Large seeds (bean, pumpkin, etc.), four for each child · Toothpicks · Glue · Green markers or crayons · Optional: small bird stickers

Preparation: Make a copy of the Storytelling Seeds picture for each child. If possible, use heavyweight paper.

Directions: Give each child a Storytelling Seeds picture and four seeds. Read the title and the writing in the first box. Ask the children what happened to the seed that fell on the pathway *(birds came and ate it)*. Let the kids glue a seed on the pathway and then draw a bird coming to eat it (or add a small bird sticker). Read the second box, and have the kids glue a seed under the rocks. Read the third box. After the kids glue the seed in that box, let them glue toothpicks (for the thorns) all around the seed. You may break the toothpicks into smaller pieces, if necessary. Read the fourth box. Have the kids glue their seed and then draw it growing into a tall, healthy plant of their choosing.

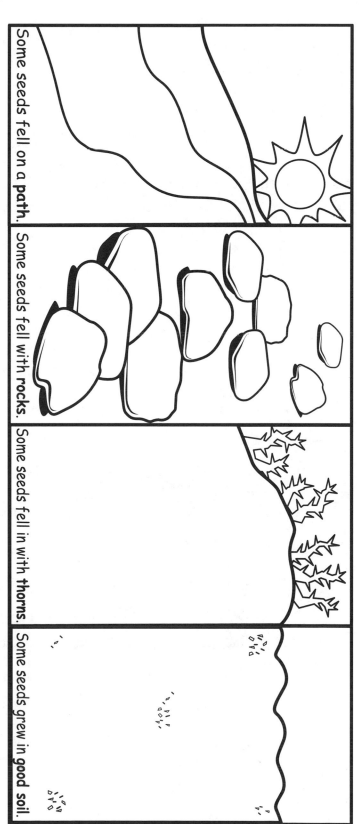

Some seeds fell on a path.

Some seeds fell with rocks.

Some seeds fell in with thorns.

Some seeds grew in good soil.

HomeLink

In Matthew 13:3-23, Jesus taught how we can grow in Him. Some people learn about Jesus, but then they don't follow Him. Some people follow Jesus for a while and then give up when problems come. These people are like the ground where the seeds fall—the birds pick up the seed, the soil is rocky or full of thorns. The seeds are like the message of God's Word.

You can be like the good soil. When the seed falls on good soil it begins to grow. Will you be like the good soil—ready to receive the message of God's Word? You can grow in your walk with Jesus by reading your Bible and talking with Jesus every day.

GCP31: Seed Mosaic

Supplies: Copies of the Seed Mosaic picture · Variety of seeds · Glue · Cardboard or poster board · Crayons

Preparation: Make a copy of the Seed Mosaic picture for each child. Glue each picture to a piece of cardboard or poster board to strengthen it.

Directions: Let the children color their picture—but not color the centers of the flowers. Spread a light layer of glue on the centers of the flowers. Let the children place seeds on the glue. Encourage them to use a variety of seeds on their pictures.

HomeLink: Matthew 13:3-23

Help your child retell the Bible story during the week, using this simplified version of the story. Your child may make the sounds indicated.

Jesus told a story about a farmer. The farmer scattered some seeds. Some fell on a path. Birds ate the seeds. (Chirp.) **Some seeds fell on rocky soil.** (Hit fist on palm of other hand.) **Some seeds fell near thorn bushes.** (Say, "Ouch!") **Other seeds fell on good soil.** (Rub hands together.) **The seeds are like the message of God's Word. The good soil is like the people who hear God's Word and understand it.**

The seeds that fell on good soil grew into plants.

The good soil is like the people who hear God's Word and understand it.

GCE32: Jesus and I Love You Card

Supplies: Copies of the card pieces and HomeLink paragraph · Construction paper (9" x 12") · Scissors · Glue · Crayons or markers · Optional: additional art supplies (glitter, lace, sequins, stamps, etc.)

Preparation: Make a copy of the card pieces for each child, as well as the HomeLink paragraph.

Directions: Give each child a copy of the card pieces and have them color them and then cut them out. Give out construction paper and glue, and show the children how to fold the paper in a card shape and where to glue the card pieces. As time permits, let the children further decorate their cards with the art supplies you have on hand.

As the children work, talk about someone they know who they want to encourage with Jesus' love. They should write that person's name on the first line of the card and then sign their own name on the bottom line. Encourage the children to show their love for this person by doing their very best work. Glue the HomeLink paragraph on the back of the card.

> **HomeLink**
>
> Today the children learned from Zacchaeus (Luke 19:1-10) that Jesus loves them so very much. He loves them no matter what they do. And He can forgive them when they do wrong.
>
> Your child made a card to tell someone that both Jesus and your child loves him or her. Help your child deliver the card to the chosen person. And reinforce today's lesson by showing your child all week long how much you love him or her.

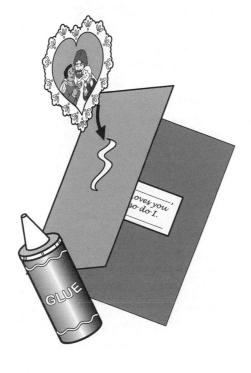

Dear _____,
Jesus Loves you
and so do I.
Love, _____

GCP32: Zaccheus Flap Picture

Supplies: Copies of the Flap Picture pieces and HomeLink · Washable markers · Scissors · Glue sticks

Preparation: Make a copy of the Flap Picture pieces and HomeLink for each child. Cut out the flaps and the figure of Jesus.

Directions: Let the children color both the picture and the flap. Show the children how to fold the flap down on the dotted line. Have them glue the flap to the picture. When the flap is opened, the picture of Jesus and Zaccheus together under the tree should be showing. Have the children close the flaps. Next, have them glue the figure of Jesus to the front of the flap book. Send home a copy of the HomeLink with each child.

HomeLink: Luke 19:1-10

Jesus showed His love to Zaccheus by forgiving him. You and your child can act out the following story during the week.

Zaccheus was a little man. Crouch down low. **He collected money from people.** Pretend to jingle coins in your hand. **Some of it he stole.** Shake your finger. **Zaccheus climbed a tree one day.** Pretend to climb a tree. **He wanted to see Jesus.** Put your hand above your eyes. **But Jesus asked him to climb down.** Pretend to climb down a tree. **Jesus planned to visit Zaccheus.** Pretend to walk and then eat. **At dinner, Zaccheus said he was sorry for taking the money. He was going to give it back.** Fold your hands in prayer. **Jesus showed His love by forgiving Zaccheus.** Give your child a hug.

GCE33: Jesus Is King Poster

Supplies: Copies of the "Jesus Is King" Poster and HomeLink · Bright colors of tissue paper · Glue · Crayons or markers · Optional: Glitter or glitter glue

Preparation: Cut tissue paper into 1¹/₂" squares. Makes copies of the "Jesus Is King" Poster and HomeLink, one for each child.

Directions: Give each child a copy of the "Jesus Is King" poster. Help children spread glue along the "J" in "Jesus." Then show them how to crumple a square of tissue paper into a small ball. Place the ball of tissue paper into the glue on the letter. Continue filling in the letter with tissue paper balls until the first letter is covered. Repeat this process for the other letters. When finished, the children may color the border. (An option is to let the children sprinkle glitter on each letter after glue is applied or they may use glitter glue to decorate the letters.) Then glue the HomeLink to the back of the poster.

HomeLink

Jesus is King!

That's what the Bible teaches in Matthew 21:1-11.

To celebrate Jesus, the people waved branches, laid their coats on the road, and shouted praises to Him. How can you praise Jesus, your King, this week? Talk about it with your family!

GCP33: Palm Branches

Supplies: Copies of the Palm Branch and HomeLink · Crayons · Green construction paper · Glue sticks · Scissors

Preparation: Make a copy of the Palm Branch and HomeLink for each child. Cut out the palm branch outlines. (If you prefer you may copy the palm branch directly onto green construction paper.)

Directions: Have the children color their Palm Branches. Help each child glue the branch to a piece of construction paper (to make the branch sturdier). Show the children how to cut or tear fringe around the edges of the branch. Then have a palm parade around your room. Let the children wave their branches and shout "Hosanna." Be sure to give a HomeLink to each child at the end of class.

HomeLink: Matthew 21:1-11

Jesus rode into Jerusalem like a king. The people waved palm branches to praise Him. Have your child use the palm branch and play-act a parade about the Bible story. You may use the following ideas.

Jesus rode on a donkey on His way to Jerusalem. Let's pretend to follow Him. People are putting coats on the road and waving branches. What will you do? People are cheering and shouting. What will you say?

GCE34: Rolling Stone Scene

Supplies: Copies of the Bible story figures · Markers or crayons · Scissors · Large sheets of construction paper (12" x 18") · Glue · Small-size, white paper plates · Paper fasteners

Preparation: Make copies of the Bible story figures, one set for each child. Make a sample of the Rolling Stone Scene for the children to follow.

Directions: Give each child a set of the Bible story figures to color and cut out. Give each child one sheet of the large construction paper, and show the children how to draw the simple outline of the cave-tomb on the right side. Then show the children where to glue the figures. (The angel sits on the tomb; the two Marys stand on the left side of the paper; the two soldiers should lie on the ground in front of the tomb.)

Have the children glue the "Jesus is alive!" sign on the tomb opening. Help the children poke a metal paper fastener through the side, not the center, of a paper plate and then through the construction paper scene by the cave-tomb. The plate should cover the tomb doorway and sign and then spin or slide over to show the stone rolling away and reveal the message.

GCP34: Resurrection Stick Puppets

Supplies: Copies of the Stick Puppets and the HomeLink · Crayons or markers · Scissors · Craft sticks (3 per child) · Tape · Resealable plastic bags

Preparation: Make a copy of the Stick Puppets and Home Story for each child. You may want to cut out the puppets before class.

Directions: Let the children color the figures of the women, the angel, and Jesus' helpers. If not already done, help the children cut them out. Help the

children tape a craft stick to the back of each figure to create the puppets. Put each child's puppets and a HomeLink in a resealable plastic bag to send home.

HomeLink: Matthew 27:33-38, 57-61; 28:1-8

Use the puppets to help your child retell the Bible story of Jesus' death and resurrection.

Some people didn't like Jesus. They had Jesus put on a cross. Jesus died. One of Jesus' friends put Jesus' body in a cave. A big rock was rolled in front of the cave as a door.

Three days later, some women went to put spices on Jesus' body. Have your child "walk" the women puppet. **They found an empty cave. An angel talked to them.** Have your child hold the angel puppet next to the women. **The angel said, "Jesus isn't here anymore. He isn't dead. He's alive again! Go tell Jesus' friends."** Hold the disciples for your child. Have your child move the women to the disciples.

Angel

The Two Marys

Jesus' Helpers

GCE35: Great Teacher Badges

Supplies: Copies of the badges and HomeLink paragraph · Markers or crayons · Scissors · Tape · Waxed paper

Preparation: Make copies of the badges on heavy paper, two for each child, and the HomeLink paragraph, one for each child.

Directions: Give each child two badges. Ask the children to think of two people who help them learn about Jesus. They should write each person's name on one of the badges. Help with spelling as necessary. The children should sign their names where indicated and color the badges. When finished, the children may cut out their badges. Roll a piece of tape and place on the back of the badge. Cover it with waxed paper. When the waxed paper is removed it will stick to the teacher's shirt.

Encourage the children to find a way to give or send the badges to the chosen teachers this week. Be sure to send a HomeLink paragraph home with each child.

HomeLink

Philip taught the Ethiopian man about Jesus (Acts 8:4-5, 26-39). Who teaches you about Jesus? Talk it over with your parents. Pray together to thank God for those people. Remember to give your Great Teacher Badges to the teachers you chose!

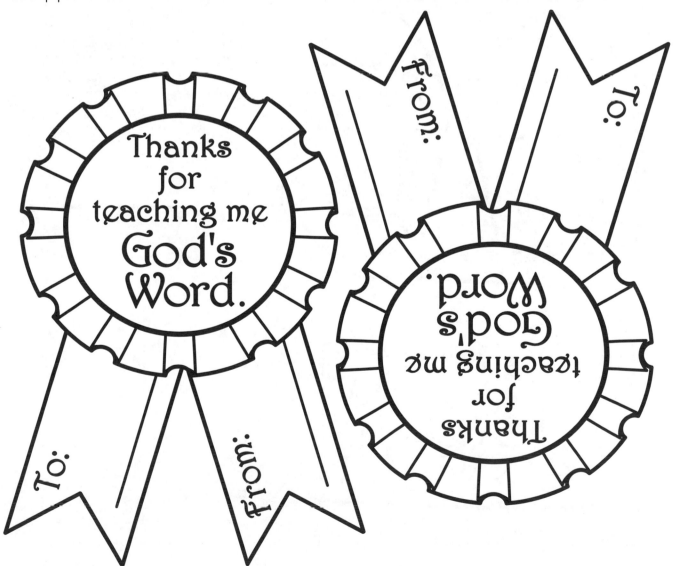

Thanks for teaching me God's Word.

To:

From:

GCP35: Bible Story Flannel Figures

Supplies: Copies of the Flannel Figures and HomeLink · Crayons · Scissors · Glue sticks · 1-inch felt squares (five per child) · Resealable plastic bags

Preparation: Make a copy of the Flannel Figures and HomeLink for each child. Cut out the pieces before class. Cut felt into 1-inch squares.

Directions: Have the children color the figures of the chariot, Philip, the man from Ethiopia, and the scroll. Help the children glue a square of felt to the back of each figure. Put two felt squares on the back of the chariot. Have the children put their flannel figures and HomeLink in a resealable plastic bag.

HomeLink: Acts 8:4-5, 26-39

Use the flannel figures to help your child retell the Bible story this week. The figures will stick to any fabric that has a little texture to it, such as the side of a sofa.

Philip was walking down the road. Have your child put the Philip figure up. **A chariot came down the road.** Have your child put the chariot near Philip. **An important man was in the chariot.** Have your child put the other man in the chariot. **What is he reading?** Put the scroll in the man's hands. **Philip asked the man if he understood what he was reading. The man asked Philip to teach him all about it.** Let your child put Philip in the chariot. **Philip told the man about Jesus.**

GCE36: Help Thumb-body Pictures

Supplies: Copies of the "Help Thumb-body" Picture · Washable inkpads or washable markers · Colored markers · Optional: damp paper towels

Preparation: Make a copy of the "Help Thumb-body" Picture for each child.

Directions: Give each child a copy of the "Help Thumb-body" Picture. Show the children how to press their thumbs on the inkpad (or color their thumbs with washable marker) and then press on the picture to make heads for the children. The children may draw the face and hair on the thumbprint to look like themselves. The children may further color the pictures as time permits. Have damp paper towels on hand for children to wipe the ink off with.

Home Link

Jesus' friends help others (Acts 9:36-41). You can show you are Jesus' friend by helping others this week. Talk with your parents about how you can be a good helper. Pray with your parents for people you can help this week. Make other thumbprint pictures at home to remind you to pray for people you can help.

GCP36: Story Flap Book

Supplies: Copies of the book panels and HomeLink · Washable markers · Stapler

Preparation: Make a copy of the three book panels and the HomeLink for each child.

Directions: Give each child a copy of the three story pictures, and let the children color them. Help the children cut apart the three story flaps on the dotted lines. Show the children how to put the books together with story flap 1 on the top and story flap 3 on the bottom. Staple each child's book together by stapling the flaps together along the top edge. Give each child a HomeLink to take home with their Story Flap Book.

HomeLink: Acts 9:36-41

Jesus' friends help others. Dorcas showed she was Jesus' friend by helping others. Peter showed he was Jesus' friend by helping Dorcas. Use the Story Flap Book to tell the Bible story to your child throughout the week.

Here is the woman named Dorcas. Have your child show you flap 1. **She loved Jesus. She helped people by making clothes for them. She became sick and died.**

Here is the man named Peter. Have your child show you flap 2. **He loved Jesus. He helped Dorcas by praying for her. He asked God to make Dorcas alive again.**

Here are Peter and Dorcas. Have your child show you flap 3. **God's power had made Dorcas come alive!**

Dorcas is Alive! ③

Peter ②

Dorcas ①

GCE37: Family Scents

Supplies: Copies of the picture frame and HomeLink · Boxes of flavored gelatin powder · Liquid glue · Small plates · Cotton swabs or toothpicks · Crayons and pencils

Preparation: Make a copy of the picture frame for each child.

Directions: Help the kids make a sweet-smelling reminder of how good it is to have a family that helps them know Jesus. Pour powdered gelatin and glue onto separate plates. Show the children how to dip a cotton swab or toothpick into the glue and spread it on one of the large letters in "FAMILY" on their paper. The kids then take a pinch of gelatin powder and sprinkle it on the glue. They may need several pinches to cover each letter. When all the letters are finished, help the children shake the excess gelatin back onto a plate. Have only a few children at a time work on the glue and gelatin while the others fill in their picture frames by drawing a picture of their family or things they love about their families.

HomeLink

In the Bible, Timothy's mom and grandmother helped him learn from God's Word (Acts 16:1-5; 2 Timothy 1:3-6; 3:14-15). Your family can help you know Jesus too. They can take you to church, read you Bible stories, and more. Say thanks to your family!

GCP37: Timothy Trading Cards

Supplies: Copies of the Trading Cards and HomeLink · Crayons · Scissors · Resealable plastic bags · Optional: cardstock

Preparation: Copy the set of six trading cards for each child. You may want to use cardstock for this craft to make the trading cards more durable. Also copy the HomeLink for each child. You may want to cut apart the cards for younger children.

Directions: Briefly talk with the children about who is on each trading card. Let each child color a set of cards. Help the children cut them apart. Place the cards and HomeLink in a resealable plastic bag and give to each child.

HomeLink: Acts 16:1–5; 2 Timothy 1:3–6; 3:14–15

Timothy's mother and grandmother helped him learn about God. Families can help us know Jesus. Use the trading cards with the following "I Spy" game to review the Bible story throughout the week. Lay all the trading cards face up to begin the game.

I spy a little boy named Timothy.

I spy a mother named Eunice. She taught Timothy about God.

I spy a grandmother named Lois. She told Timothy stories from God's book.

I spy God's Book.

I spy Timothy all grown up.

I spy Paul. Timothy helped Paul teach people about Jesus.

YOUNG TIMOTHY

PAUL

TIMOTHY

LOIS

BIBLE SCROLL

EUNICE

GCE38: Teamwork Paper People

Supplies: 1 copy of the paper person per child and HomeLink · Colored pencils

Directions: Give each child a paper person. Be sure each child puts his or her name at the top where indicated before starting. Tell the children that they will work together to complete their paper person. Have the children listen carefully to the directions. Make sure each child is finished before proceeding to the next direction. Have the kids sign their name by the part they draw on each paper.

1. Hand your paper to the child on your left and draw in the face of the person (eyes, nose, mouth).

2. Hand the paper to the child on your left and draw hair on the person.

3. Hand the paper to the next child to the left and draw a shirt. You may decorate the shirt.

4. Hand the paper to the next child to the left and draw pants on the person.

5. Return the paper to the child whose name is at the top.

> **HomeLink**
>
> Working together is fun! It's also what Jesus' friends do. Hang up your Teamwork Paper Person at home where it will remind you to work together with others. Take time to read the names of the kids who helped draw the body parts. It's fun to work together, and it's what pleases Jesus. Try this activity at home with your family to remind you to work together.

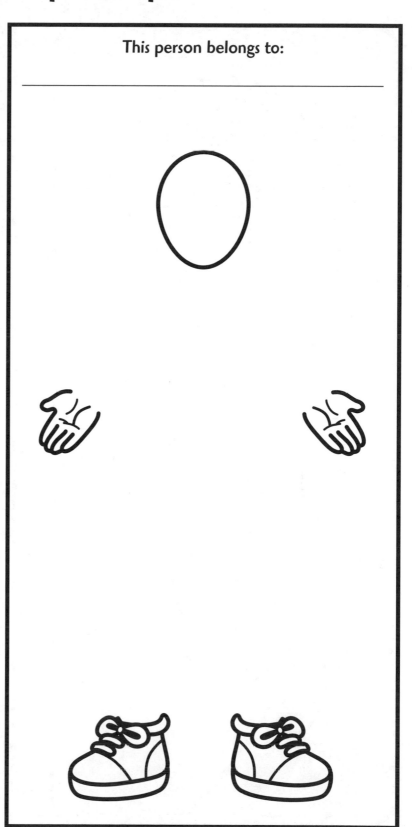

This person belongs to:

_____

GCP38: Doorknob Hanger

My Friend Jesus

Supplies: Copies of the Doorknob Hanger and HomeLink · Washable markers · Scissors · Glue

Preparation: Make a copy of the Doorknob Hanger and HomeLink for each child. Cut out the doorknob hangers and the HomeLink. For younger children, carefully cut on the dashed line, and remove the circle from each doorknob hanger.

Directions: Read the doorknob hanger to the children. Show them how it hangs on a doorknob. Let each child color a doorknob hanger. Help the children cut them out on the dotted line and remove the circle. Let each child glue the HomeLink to the back of his or her hanger.

HomeLink: Acts 11:20-26

Barnabas and Paul worked together to teach the Christians in Antioch. The following story is one way you can review the Bible story with your child throughout the week.

Here is the city of Antioch. Hold your hands together as if making a roof.

Here are many people who believe in Jesus. Shake your fingers.

Who can help them learn more about Jesus?

Here is Barnabas. He will teach the people. Hold up one finger.

Here are many people who believe in Jesus. Shake your fingers.

Barnabas needs someone to help him teach the people. Who can help Barnabas?

Here is Paul. He will help Barnabas teach the people. Hold up another finger.

GCE39: Megaphone for Jesus

Supplies: Copies of the stickers and HomeLink · Crayons and markers · Scissors · Construction paper (12" x 18") · Clear tape · Glue sticks · Glitter glue

Preparation: Copy a set of stickers and the HomeLink Cheer for each child.

Directions: The children will each make a megaphone to remind them to tell their friends about Jesus. Give each child a set of stickers to color. Then have the children cut them out, along with the cheer.

Show the children how to roll a sheet of construction paper into a megaphone—small at one end and large at the other. Make sure the kids don't roll it too tightly. Tape the megaphones so they can't unroll. Help the children trim the large end so it is even. Let the kids glue on their four stickers and the HomeLink Cheer. They may further decorate their megaphones with glitter glue.

When finished, let the children practice using their megaphone to tell a classmate about Jesus.

HomeLink

Cheer

Two, four, six, eight!

Paul told friends that Jesus is great!

Eight, six, four, two!

Tell your friends He loves them too!

(Acts 18:1-4, 24-28)

Talk together as a family to find ways to tell friends and neighbors about Jesus.

GCP39: Tent Sewing Cards

Supplies: Copies of the tent and HomeLink ·
Cardstock · Hole punch · Yarn · Masking tape · Glue ·
Optional: Crayons

Preparation: Make a copy of the tent on cardstock for
each child. Also make a copy of the HomeLink for each
child. Cut out the tents, and use a hole punch to punch
holes where indicated. Cut a three-foot length of yarn
for each child. Wrap tape around one end of yarn as a
"needle." Tape the other end to the back of the tent.

Directions: Remind the children that Paul and his new
friends, Aquila and Priscilla, were tentmakers. Give each
child a prepared tent. Show the children how to bring
their needle up one hole and down the next to "sew"
the tent. Encourage the children to sew all the way
around their tents. When finished, let each child glue a
copy of the HomeLink to the back of his or her tent. If
time permits, let the children color their tents.

HomeLink: Acts 18:1-4, 24-28

Jesus wants us to tell our friends about Him. Paul
told his friends, Aquila and Priscilla, about Jesus.
Then Aquila and Priscilla told their friend Apollos
about Jesus. Use the following skit throughout the
week to help your child review the Bible story.

Aquila and Priscilla made tents. (Let your
child pretend to sew the tent.)

Paul was their friend. (Hug your child.) **Paul
made tents too.**

Paul told Aquila and Priscilla about Jesus.
(Make a cross with your fingers.)

**Aquila and Priscilla made a new friend
named Apollos.** (Shake hands.)

They told him about Jesus. (Make a cross with
your fingers.)

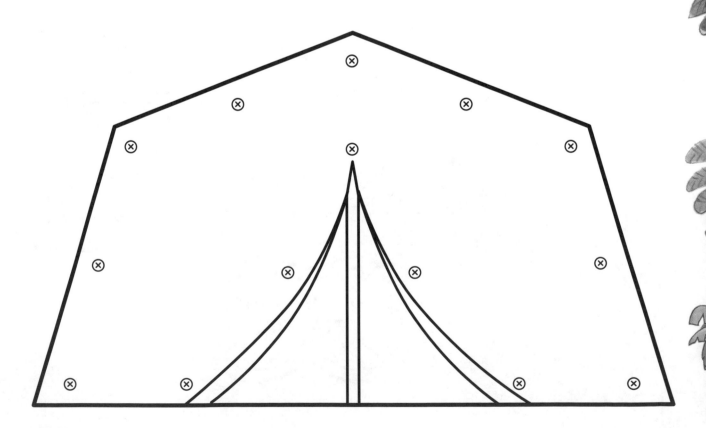

GCE40: Scratch and Sniff Art

Supplies: Copy of fruit picture for each child and HomeLink · Two packages of fruit flavored gelatin (different flavors) · Watercolor paints · Water · Small bowls or plastic tubs · Small paintbrushes · Craft glue · Cotton-tipped swabs

Directions: Let the kids paint the fruit picture with watercolors. Let it dry. When the pictures are dry, spread a little craft glue with a cotton-tipped swab on the "fruit." Sprinkle a little fruit flavored gelatin over the wet glue. When the glue dries, the children can "scratch and sniff" their pictures.

HomeLink

What's your favorite fruit? Think about what it tastes like, smells like, looks like, and feels like. Didn't God make great fruit?! Use this picture to remind you of all the wonderful fruits and other foods that God made. If you made this picture with the special directions your teacher gave you, you'll be able to "scratch and sniff" your picture. When you get home, put this picture in your kitchen or dining room to remind you of one way that God takes care of you.

GCP40: Manna Color and Glue Picture

Supplies: Copy of the coloring page for each child and HomeLink · Crayons · Glue · Uncooked white rice

Preparation: Make a copy of the coloring page for each child, with the HomeLink.

Directions: Have each child color his or her picture except for the ground and the inside of the baskets. (Glue does not stick well to crayon.) Show the children how to put dots of glue on the ground area of the picture and then drop rice on the glue. Explain that the rice represents manna.

HomeLink: At Noah's Park Children's Church, your child is learning that God takes care of us. This week, your child learned that God took care of the Israelites by giving them food (Exodus 16:11-18). Do this action story with your child this week.

The Israelites and Moses were in the desert. They were walking to their new land. Move your feet in place as if walking. **But there wasn't any food. They were hungry.** Rub your stomach. **God promised to give them food. One evening He sent birds, called quail, for them to eat.** Pretend to eat. **Every morning God sent a food called manna. The people gathered it in baskets.** Pretend to put manna in a basket. **God took care of the Israelites. God takes care of us.**

GCE41: Rock Painting

Supplies: Assorted shapes and sizes of smooth rocks · Poster or acrylic paints (in blue, white, and more colors if available) · Small paintbrushes · Water to clean paint off brushes · Paint shirts · Old newspapers or table coverings · Copies of HomeLink paragraph, one for each child

Preparation: Wash and dry rocks so the surfaces are clean for painting. (The rocks must be thoroughly dry.) Make a copy of HomeLink paragraph for each child.

Directions: Set out the supplies where children can reach them. Let each child choose a rock to decorate. Remind the kids of how God produced water from a rock for His people. Talk with the children about how they might paint their rocks to look like water or any other image that reminds them of the Bible story. The children may paint designs, words, or just cover the rock in blue and white to represent rushing water. Have the Park Patrol on hand to help with spills and to interact with the children. Ask them how their painted rocks remind them of today's Bible story.

HomeLink

Water from a rock? How can that be? It's amazing!

Kids, be sure to tell today's Bible story to your parents. They'll be amazed too. Here's a little help:

Moses led the people of Israel through the desert. They came to a place where there was NO water. The people needed water. The animals needed water. Everyone complained. Except Moses. Moses prayed.

God told Moses to go to a special rock. Moses should hit the rock with his walking stick. Moses trusted God. So Moses did what God said. Moses went to the special rock. He hit it with his walking stick.

Water gushed out of the rock! Lots of water! The people had water. The animals had water. God showed that He cared about His people.

God cares about us, too. His gift of water is just one way that God shows He cares.

GCP41: God Takes Care of Us Cup Holders

Supplies: Copy of Cup Holder and HomeLink for each child · 5-ounce cup for each child (paper or plastic) · Crayons · Scissors · Glue sticks · Tape · Optional: cardstock

Preparation: Make a copy of the Cup Holder and HomeLink for each child. Cut out the HomeLink and save to hand out at the end of class. If you have younger children, cut out the cup holder. As an option, you may reinforce the cup holders by tracing the pattern onto the cardstock and gluing the cup holders onto the cardstock before cutting out.

Directions: Invite the children to color their cup holders. Crayons will work best for this project because the color won't run if the project gets wet. Show the children how to glue the cup holder together on the "glue here" tabs. Give each child a paper or plastic cup to put in his or her cup holder. (If the cupholder won't stay in place, you can tape it to the cup with a small piece of tape.) As you pass out the cups, talk with the children about how water was used in today's Bible story.

HomeLink: Exodus 17:1-6

God takes care of us. Just as He provided water for the Israelites in the wilderness, God still provides for us today. To help your child remember the Bible story, act out the following story at home during the week. Your child will need something for a walking stick and a rock.

Moses and the people of Israel were in the desert. Have your child walk around with the walking stick. **They didn't have any water. God told Moses to walk ahead to a special rock.** Have your child walk to the rock. **God told Moses to hit the rock with his stick.** Ask your child to tap the rock with the stick. **What came out of the rock?** Let your child shout, *"Water!"* Water for everyone to drink. **God took care of Moses and the people of Israel. God takes care of us.**

GCE42: Dough Art

Supplies: Play dough or art clay · Cardboard piece · Copy of HomeLink paragraph for each child

Preparation: Buy or make play dough or art clay (see recipe below). Make copies of HomeLink paragraph.

Directions: Provide each child with a chunk of play dough or clay.

Encourage the children to make something that symbolizes themselves, such as their face, their whole selves, or the letters of their name. Talk about how God takes care of each of them and loves them.

When finished, have the children place their creation on a piece of cardboard to take home. Give each child a copy of the HomeLink paragraph to take home as well. Tell the children to let the dough air dry at home, and after that they may paint it with tempera paints or markers.

Play Dough Recipe

2 c. flour

1 c. salt

4 T. cream of tartar

1 pkg. unsweetened dry drink mix for scent and color

2 c. warm water

2 T. cooking oil

Stir over medium heat until mixture pulls away from sides to form a ball. Store in airtight container. (For eight to ten children.)

HomeLink

You are special to God, and God takes care of you. There are many ways He does this. One way is through His plans. God has wonderful plans that we can be a part of. God wants to be a part of your daily plans too.

Talk with your parents about your plans for this week. Pray together. Ask God to help you make plans that please Him. Use your play dough art to remind you of yourself—and that God takes care of you!

GCP42: Abraham and Sarah Stand-up Figures

Supplies: Set of Bible Figures and HomeLink for each child · Crayons or colored pencils · Scissors · Tape · Resealable plastic bags · Optional: fabric scraps, glue

Preparation: Make a copy of the Stand-up Bible Figures and the HomeLink for each child. Cut the HomeLink from each page. You may want to cut out the figures for younger children before class.

Directions: Let the children color the figures. As an option, you may let the children glue on fabric scraps. Show the children how to fold back the tabs on the dotted lines to make each figure stand. Give each child a resealable plastic bag to keep the HomeLink paragraph and figures together.

HomeLink: Genesis 12:1-9

Today your child learned that God took care of Abraham and his family when they traveled to a new land. Let your child set up the figures as you tell the following story during the week.

God told Abraham to move. Set out the Abraham figure. **God promised to give Abraham many blessings. Abraham's wife, Sarah, packed.** Set out the Sarah figure. **Abraham's nephew Lot packed.** Set out the Lot figure. **Abraham's helpers packed.** Set out the figure of the helpers and sheep. **They all traveled to the new land God had waiting for them.** Move the figures as if traveling. **They thanked God for taking care of them. Then Abraham and Sarah unpacked.** Pick up the figures of Abraham and Sarah. **Lot and the helpers unpacked too.** Pick up the figures of Lot and the helpers.

GCE43: Promise Keeper Pouch

Supplies: Heavy construction paper · Scissors · Glue · Yarn or ribbon · Hole punch · Art supplies (glitter, markers, stickers, etc.) · Slips of paper · Copies of "God Keeps His Promises" paragraph

Preparation: Cut construction paper into 4" x 8" rectangles. Make a sample of the pouch for the children to follow. Make copies of the "God Keeps His Promises" paragraph, one for each child. An option is to copy the "God Keeps His Promises" paragrph and retangular shape directly onto colored construction paper.

Directions: Have the children fold their rectangular paper in half to make a square. They should glue the two sides together, leaving open the end opposite the fold. Punch a hole on each side of the opening so the children may thread yarn or ribbon (approximately 20" long) through and knot it. You may want to glue down the knots for extra security.

Children glue the "God Keeps His Promises" paragraphs on their pouches. (If you chose to copy the paragraph and rectangular shape directly onto construction paper, you will eliminate this step.) Then they may decorate their pouches with art supplies. On slips of paper, kids can write or draw promises God keeps and insert them in the pouch. They can add to the pouch whenever they learn a new promise of God's.

HomeLink

God keeps His promises!

God made great promises to Abraham and Sarah. And God kept His promises! God makes great promises to us in the Bible. And God keeps those promises too!

Write down some of God's promises. Keep them in this Promise Keeper Pouch. Talk about God's promises with your parents. Thank God for His promises.

GCP43: God Cares for Me Visor

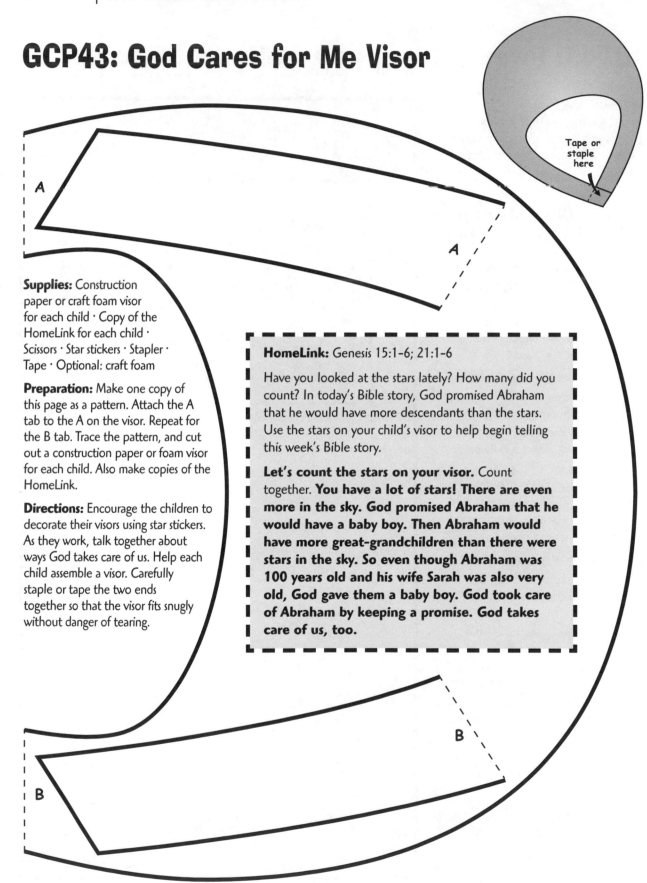

Tape or staple here

Supplies: Construction paper or craft foam visor for each child · Copy of the HomeLink for each child · Scissors · Star stickers · Stapler · Tape · Optional: craft foam

Preparation: Make one copy of this page as a pattern. Attach the A tab to the A on the visor. Repeat for the B tab. Trace the pattern, and cut out a construction paper or foam visor for each child. Also make copies of the HomeLink.

Directions: Encourage the children to decorate their visors using star stickers. As they work, talk together about ways God takes care of us. Help each child assemble a visor. Carefully staple or tape the two ends together so that the visor fits snugly without danger of tearing.

HomeLink: Genesis 15:1-6; 21:1-6

Have you looked at the stars lately? How many did you count? In today's Bible story, God promised Abraham that he would have more descendants than the stars. Use the stars on your child's visor to help begin telling this week's Bible story.

Let's count the stars on your visor. Count together. **You have a lot of stars! There are even more in the sky. God promised Abraham that he would have a baby boy. Then Abraham would have more great-grandchildren than there were stars in the sky. So even though Abraham was 100 years old and his wife Sarah was also very old, God gave them a baby boy. God took care of Abraham by keeping a promise. God takes care of us, too.**

GCE44: Batik Art

Supplies: Copy of "God Cares for Me" for each child · Crayons · Watercolor paints (or water tinted with food coloring drops) · Paintbrushes · Old newspaper or table coverings

Preparation: Make a copy of this page for each child.

Directions for Kids: God took care of Elijah (1 Kings 17). God takes care of you, too. He has a lot of ways to do that. Use crayons to draw some ways that God takes care of you. Maybe you can draw some very important people in your life. Or maybe you can draw a bunch of important things that God has given you.

It is important to color hard with your crayon. Darker colors show up better than lighter colors. After you draw with crayons, paint over the WHOLE picture with watercolor paint. It'll leave your picture looking cool—like batik art.

GOD CARES FOR ME!

GCP44: Elijah Hand Puppet

Supplies: Copies of Elijah pattern and HomeLink · Paper lunch bags · Scissors · Glue sticks · Washable markers

Preparation: Make a copy of the Elijah pattern and HomeLink for each child. For younger children, you may want to cut out the puppet pieces before class.

Directions: Let the children color the face and body of Elijah and cut them out. With the bags upside down (the open end at the bottom), help the children glue the face of Elijah on the top, folded end of the bag. Then help the children glue the body onto the side of the bag just under where the end is folded over. Have each child glue a copy of the HomeLink to the back of the puppet. To work the puppets, put your hand in the bag with your four fingers curled into the bottom folded part. Move your fingers up and down a little to make the puppet "talk."

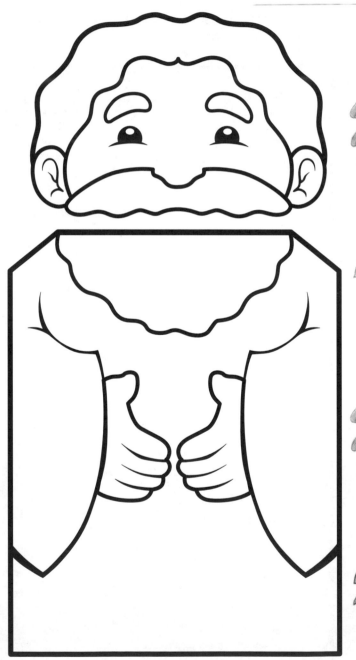

> **HomeLink:** 1 Kings 17:8-26
>
> God took care of Elijah by having a widow share her bread with him. Let your child use this Elijah puppet to retell the story to you. You might use these questions to help your child tell it.
>
> **What was the problem in Elijah's land?** *(There was no rain and everyone was hungry.)* **God told Elijah to go to a certain woman. What did he ask her to do?** *(Share her water and bread.)* **What did the woman tell Elijah about the flour and oil that she used to make bread?** *(That she didn't have enough.)* **What did Elijah promise?** *(That God would give her flour and oil for bread until the rains started again.)* **What happened?** *(The woman shared, and she always had enough flour and oil.)*

GCE45: Get Along Board Game

Supplies: Crayons or markers · Index cards · Metal fasteners · Paper clips · Photocopies of game board · Game markers

Directions: First let the children color their game boards. They may choose to add illustrations of themselves and friends and family at appropriate spaces. Hand out index cards, metal fasteners, and paper clips. Help the children draw one horizontal and one vertical line to divide an index card into four equal spaces. The kids should number each space, one through four. Attach the paper clip as the spinner by pushing the paper fastener through the card where the lines intersect. Allow time for the children to play the game with friends, following the directions on the game board.

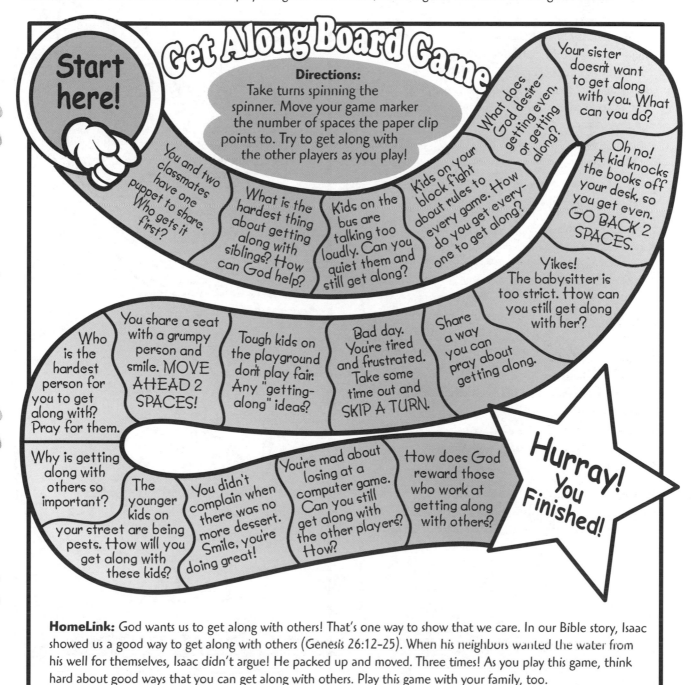

HomeLink: God wants us to get along with others! That's one way to show that we care. In our Bible story, Isaac showed us a good way to get along with others (Genesis 26:12-25). When his neighbors wanted the water from his well for themselves, Isaac didn't argue! He packed up and moved. Three times! As you play this game, think hard about good ways that you can get along with others. Play this game with your family, too.

GCP45: Hand Puppets

Supplies: Copies of the Isaac hand puppet and HomeLink · Markers · White paper · Scissors · Clear tape · Yarn scraps · Glue sticks

Preparation: Make copies of the Isaac hand puppet and HomeLink for each child. Cut them out.

Directions: Have the children color both sides of the puppet. You could let the children glue yarn scraps on the puppets for hair. Show the children how to fold their puppets on the dotted line. Carefully tape the edges of the puppet together. Let the children wear their puppets to talk about ways they can help others. Be sure to include a HomeLink with each puppet at the end of class.

HomeLink: Genesis 26:12-25

In today's Bible story, Isaac's neighbors didn't want to share. Isaac dug wells to find water, but his neighbors wanted the wells instead. God showed Isaac how to get along with these neighbors. Isaac chose not to argue with them; instead he moved. Let your child use this puppet to retell the Bible story. You may use this skit to help. You might use small building blocks to create the well where indicated.

Show me Isaac and his well. Your child should build a well from blocks and put the Isaac puppet by it.

Isaac's neighbors asked him to move. Can you build a new well for Isaac? Have your child build another well and put Isaac by it.

Isaac's new neighbors wanted him to move again. Can you build another new well for Isaac? Your child should build a third well and put Isaac by it.

God was happy with Isaac. Isaac chose not to argue.

Show me the other side of your puppet. Now I see a puppet of you! How can you get along with someone today?

GCE46: Forgiveness Bookmark

Supplies: Cardstock · Crayons or marker · Any craft items on hand (stickers, glitter, etc.) · Optional: paper punch · Optional: yarn or narrow ribbon

Preparation: On cardstock, make a copy of the "Forgive Others" bookmark for each child.

Directions: Give out the supplies, and encourage the children to each decorate their own bookmark as a reminder to forgive others. (They should decorate the plain side of their bookmark.) If the children would like ideas, you might suggest they draw a cross, a picture of today's Bible story about Joseph, or include today's memory verse. Remind the children to read the "Forgive Others" paragraph that is on the back of their bookmarks. As an option, punch a hole about half an inch from the top of the bookmark and thread through a piece of yarn or ribbon. Chat with children about forgiveness and how they can use their bookmark as a reminder to forgive.

FORGIVE OTHERS

Joseph's brothers were very mean to him. (Genesis 37:27-28)

But Joseph forgave them and helped them. (Genesis 45:1-15)

God wants all of us to forgive others and care for them. It's God's way!

Talk to your parents about today's Bible story and what you have learned about forgiveness.
This week look for ways to be kind to others.
If someone is mean to you, forgive them just as Joseph forgave his brothers.

GCP46: Joseph Story Cards

Supplies: Copies of Joseph Story Cards and HomeLink · Crayons · Scissors · Tape

Preparation: Make a copy of the Joseph Story Cards and HomeLink for each child.

Directions: Let the children color the four Story Cards.

As they work, talk about each picture. Help the children cut the four pictures apart. Let the children practice putting the Story Cards in order. Fold the HomeLink section on the dotted line. Tape the two sides. Then place the Story Cards into the pocket to take home at the end of class.

HomeLink: Genesis 37:27-28; 45:1-15

One way that God teaches us to care for others is to forgive them. That is what your child learned in the story of Joseph and his brothers today. Let your child use the Joseph Story Cards to retell the Bible story during the week, with your help.

Can you find the picture of the boy named Joseph? His father loved him very much. His brothers didn't like him.

Joseph's brothers sold Joseph to men who took him to Egypt. Joseph worked hard in Egypt. Where is the picture of the men and their camels?

Joseph worked for the king of Egypt. What did Joseph look like then? Joseph made sure people had food to eat.

Joseph's brothers came to buy some food. Show me what Joseph did when he saw his brothers. God taught Joseph to care for others by forgiving his brothers.

GCE47: Kindness Calendars

Supplies: Photocopies of the Kindness Calendar and HomeLink · Crayons or markers · Pencils · Tape or glue · Scissors

Preparation: Make a copy of the Kindness Calendar and HomeLink for each child.

Directions: Pass out the calendars and let the children look at them. Read together the days of the week. Briefly discuss how the calendar can help the children look for people to show kindness to each day this week. There is a box to check off each day, and space to write or draw how they helped someone that day. Tape or glue the HomeLink paragraph to the back of the calendar.

HomeLink

You can look up this week's Bible story with your mom or dad and read it together: 2 Samuel 4:4; 9:1-13. Then use this Kindness Calendar to remind you all week long to look for people to be kind to. Write or draw how you helped someone on each day of the week.

Sunday ☐ A Friend	
Monday ☐ Family Member or Relative	
Tuesday ☐ A neighbor	
Wednesday ☐ Classmate or Teacher	
Thursday ☐ Someone Older	
Friday ☐ A Needy Person	
Saturday ☐ Someone Younger	

MY KINDNESS CALENDAR

GCP47: Care Bears

Supplies: Copies of the Care Bear and HomeLink · Crayons · Tissue paper, paper towels, or bathroom tissue · Tape or stapler and staples

Preparation: Make a copy of the Care Bear and HomeLink for each child. For younger children, cut them out.

Directions: Have the children color their Care Bears and cut them out. As they are working, read the words on the heart. Talk about ways the children might show kindness to others this week. Help the children tape or staple the edges of the bear together, leaving the bottom open. Let the children lightly stuff the bear; then staple the bottom edges together. Pass out the HomeLink to go home with the bear.

HomeLink: 2 Samuel 4:4; 9:1-13

King David showed kindness to Mephibosheth [muh-FIB-oh-sheth]. Retell the Bible story with your child during the week using these motions:

King David loved God. (Make a crown with your hands.) **David wanted to keep a promise to the old king's family. King David** (make a crown) **wanted to show kindness to that family. There was one grandson left. He was a young man, but he couldn't walk very well. His name was Mephibosheth.** (Point to your feet.) **King David** (make a crown) **gave Mephibosheth** (point to your feet) **new land. King David** (make a crown) **invited Mephibosheth** (point to your feet) **to live near him and eat with him.**

God cares and so do I.

GCE48: Helping Idea Cube

In Your School

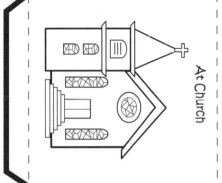

At Church

A Senior Citizen

A Child Crying at the School Playground

A Family Member

A neighbor

Supplies: Copies of the cube pattern and HomeLink paragraph · Markers or crayons · Scissors · Tape

Preparation: Make copies of the cube pattern and the HomeLink paragraph, one for each child.

Directions: Let the children color their cubes. Ask them to draw a picture of a family member on the blank square. Help them fold on all the dashed lines and assemble the cube. Tape the tabs to make the cube stay together. To play with the cube, the kids toss their cubes on the table or floor. According to the picture that lands facing up, they think up a creative and useful way to help the person pictured. Send home a HomeLink paragraph with each child.

GCP48: Bible Story Magnets

Supplies: Copies of the figures (below) and HomeLink · Colored pencils or crayons · Scissors · Magnetic tape with adhesive backing · Resealable plastic bags

Preparation: Make a copy of the Bible Story Magnet figures and the HomeLink for each child. Use heavy-stock paper for the figures. For younger children, cut them out. Cut one-inch lengths of magnetic tape, five pieces for each child.

Directions: Let each child color a set of Bible Story Magnet figures. If not already done, help the children cut them out. Then give out the magnetic tape pieces. Help each child remove the adhesive backing from one piece at a time and attach it to the back of a figure to make it a magnet. Have each child put his or her set of Bible Story Magnets and a HomeLink in a resealable plastic bag.

HomeLink: 2 Kings 4:1-7

God directed Elisha to help a poor widow and her two sons. God did a big thing using a little thing—a simple jar of oil. By retelling the story with Bible Story Magnets, your child can think about how he or she might help others in little ways that might end up making a big difference. Have your child use the figures to act out the following story during the week. The figures will stick to a refrigerator door, a baking sheet, or any metal surface.

Here is a poor woman. Have your child put up the figure of the widow. **She has to pay a lot of money. But she doesn't have money. The woman went to Elisha.** Have your child put the Elisha magnet next to the widow. **He told her to pour water from her little jar into lots of big jars.** Have your child put the single jar near the woman's hand. Set the group of jars next to the woman. **Elisha told the woman to sell the extra jars of oil. The woman had enough money to pay what she owed and buy food for her family.** Your child may put the sons next to the woman.

GCE49: Tools of Clay

Supplies: Play dough or modeling clay or use the recipe below · Tools for shaping clay (plastic knives, rollers, etc.) · Waxed paper or foil squares · Copies of the HomeLink paragraph

Preparation: Make a copy of the HomeLink paragraph to be sent home with each child.

Directions: Tell the children that most jobs use some kind of tool. Show the children the tools you brought to work with clay. Then have the kids think of a job God has given them and make up a tool to go with it. For example, children's "jobs" may include going to school, being an obedient child, learning about Jesus, or doing certain chores or responsibilities. Encourage creative thinking in what type of tool they might create out of clay. Place their finished tools on squares of waxed paper or foil.

HomeLink: Kid Jobs

Talk about these questions with your parents.

What are your jobs as a kid?

Which jobs do you like best?

What "tools" do you use in your jobs?

How can you please God with your jobs?

Read the Bible story again with your parents, Acts 6:1-7, and talk about jobs that people in your church have.

Play Dough Recipe

2 c. flour

1 c. salt

4 T. cream of tartar

1 pkg. unsweetened dry drink mix for scent and color

2 c. warm water

2 T. cooking oil

Stir over medium heat until mixture pulls away from sides to form a ball. Store in airtight container. (For eight to ten children.)

GCP49: Caring Coupon Books

Supplies: Copies of the Caring Coupon Book and HomeLink · Scissors · Colored pencils or crayon · Stapler and staples

Preparation: Make a copy of the Caring Coupons and HomeLink for each child. For younger children, cut apart the eight coupon book pages and the HomeLink.

Directions: Help the children cut apart the coupons on the solid lines. Let the children color their coupons. As they color, talk about how they can use the coupons during the week. Show the children how to put their books together with the cover on the top, followed by the introductory page and then the coupons. Staple the left edges together for the children. Send home a copy of HomeLink with each Caring Coupon Book.

HomeLink: Acts 6:1-7

In today's Bible story, the church gives a special job to seven men so that widows won't be neglected. These men show God's caring. Talk with your child about how to use the Caring Coupon Book throughout the week. Also review the Bible story with your child:

The Bible tells us that some women needed help. Make a book with your hands. **They were very hungry.** Rub your tummy. **The teachers of the church had a way to help them. They chose seven men.** Hold up seven fingers. **These men would help the women by giving them food to eat. The teachers of the church prayed for the seven men.** Fold your hands. **Then the seven men took care of the women.**

Your child can "spend" these coupons by doing caring or helpful things for others. Each time your child does something kind, let him or her give a coupon to the recipient of the act.

I ♥ Caring for You!

I ♥ Caring for You!

I ♥ Caring for You!

I ♥ Caring for You!

My Little Book of CARING COUPONS

I ♥ Caring for You!

I ♥ Caring for You!

GCE50: Paper People

Supplies: Copies of Paper People pattern and HomeLink paragraph · Scissors · Crayons · Construction Paper

Preparation: Make a copy of the HomeLink paragraph and Paper People pattern (below) for each child.

Directions: Give each child a copy of the Paper People pattern. Help the children fold the construction paper as shown in the picture below. Place the Paper People pattern on the folded construction paper, then cut on the solid lines. Remind the children not to cut on folded edges. Then have the children color and decorate their row of Paper People so that each person looks different, since Jesus loves so many different kinds of people. Give each child a copy of the HomeLink paragraph to take home.

> **HomeLink**
>
> Jesus cared for Matthew, the tax collector, even though the Pharisees looked down on him (Matthew 9:9-13). In fact, Jesus cares for everyone. The Paper People can remind you of how many different kinds of people Jesus cares about. Talk with your parents about some neighbors or classmates who are different from you. Talk about how to show Jesus' care for them. Pray together for those people. Thank Jesus for caring for you, too!

FOLD

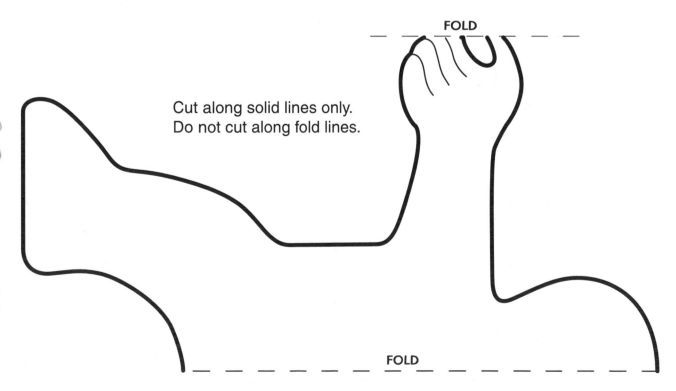

Cut along solid lines only.
Do not cut along fold lines.

FOLD

GCP50: Matthew and Jesus Finger Puppets

Supplies: Copies of the puppets and HomeLink · Crayons · Scissors · Resealable plastic bags · Optional: cardstock, fabric scraps, and glue

Preparation: Make a copy of the Matthew and Jesus puppets and the HomeLink for each child. You may want to use cardstock for the puppets to make them more durable. Cut out the puppets and the finger holes.

Directions: Give each child a Matthew and a Jesus puppet to color. If you chose to use cardstock, the children could also glue on fabric scraps to decorate them. When completed, show the children how to put the finger puppets on their fingers and make them walk. (The index and middle fingers go through the holes to become the legs of the puppet.) Put each child's puppets and a HomeLink in a resealable plastic bag to send home.

HomeLink: Matthew 9:9-13

Jesus called the tax collector, Matthew, to follow Him. During the week, let your child help you retell this Bible story using the puppets. Encourage your child to add some dialogue.

Who is the man who collects people's money? His name is Matthew. People call him a sinner because he steals money. Your child should use the Matthew puppet.

Who is walking by Matthew? His name is Jesus. He wants Matthew to stop stealing. Jesus wants Matthew to be one of His helpers. Your child should use the Jesus puppet.

Jesus cared for Matthew. Let your child walk the two puppets together. **Jesus cares for everyone.**

GCE51: Love Your Neighbor Maze

Directions for Kids: Do you know how to love your neighbor? Who is your neighbor? Look for clues as you do this maze. At the end write the sentence in the correct order. Then decorate the page. Draw pictures of people you could show Jesus' love to. Remember, care for others as Jesus cares for you.

My neighbor is:

_____ _____ _____

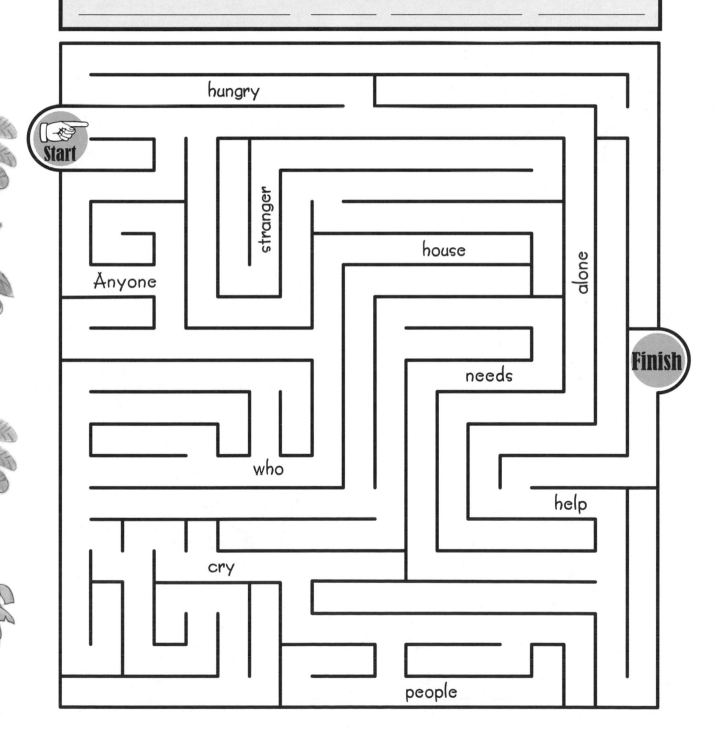

GCP51: Good Samaritan Flannel Figures

Supplies: Copies of flannel figures and HomeLink · Crayons · Scissors · Glue sticks · 1" flannel squares (four per child) · Resealable plastic bags

Preparation: Make a copy of the four Bible story figures and the HomeLink for each child. Cut out the figures and the HomeLink. Cut four one-inch flannel squares for each child.

Directions: Have each child color a set of story figures. Show the children how to glue a square of flannel on the back of each figure. Help the children put their figures and a HomeLink in resealable plastic bags.

HomeLink: Luke 10:25-37

In Jesus' story of the Good Samaritan, He taught that we should show love and care to everyone around us. Use the following story to help your child review the Bible story. The flannel figures will stick to textured fabrics, like a sofa.

One day Jesus told a story. The story taught that Jesus wants us to care for everyone:

A man was walking down a road. Some bad men stole his money and hurt him. They left him by the road. Have your child show the hurt man. **A priest saw the man, but he walked right by.** Have your child move the priest past the man. **Then a Levite came. He walked by the man too.** Have your child move the Levite past the man. **Finally, a man from another country, a Samaritan, walked down the road.** Have your child move the Samaritan to the man. **He stopped by the hurt man. The Samaritan helped the man and put him on his donkey.** Have your child put the hurt man on the donkey. **The Samaritan took the hurt man to a place where he could get better.**

Priest

Hurt Man

Samaritan and his Donkey

Levite

GCE52: Thank You Journal

Supplies: Copies of the journal page and HomeLink paragraph · Scissors · Construction paper · White copy paper · Stapler · Colored pencils or markers · Optional: stickers

Preparation: Make a copy of the journal page and HomeLink paragraph for each child. Cut them out.

Directions: Briefly discuss what a journal is (a place where you can write or draw your thoughts). Explain that the children will each make a journal to keep track of ways Jesus has cared for them and things to thank Him for.

Give each child a piece of construction paper (6" x 9") to fold in half for the covers, and a few sheets of white copy paper for inside. Help the children put them in a neat stack with the "Thanks" page on top. Have them insert all the pages into the construction paper cover and staple the book three times along the left edge.

The children may decorate their covers with markers and stickers. They can write "My Thank You Journal" on the front cover. Give each child a HomeLink paragraph to glue inside the front cover.

Encourage the children to make their first entry in the journal, writing down a few words or a sentence (depending on their writing level) or drawing a picture.

HomeLink

Jesus is happy when we remember to thank Him (Luke 17:11-19).

How does Jesus show His care for you? What can you thank Him for?

Every day, look for Jesus' love for you. And every day, draw or write your thanks to Him in this journal.

GCP52: Bible Story Stick Puppets

Supplies: Copies of the faces and HomeLink · Colored pencils · Glue sticks or tape · Scissors · Craft sticks (10 for each child) · Resealable plastic bags

Preparation: Make copies of the faces below, one set of 10 for each child. Cut out the faces. Also copy the HomeLink for each child.

Directions: Give each child a set of 10 faces, and let the children color them. Help the children glue or tape the 10 faces to 10 craft sticks. Show the children how to use the stick puppets to retell the Bible story. Send each child's set of puppets and HomeLink home in a resealable plastic bag.

HomeLink: Luke 17:11-19

Jesus cared for the 10 men with leprosy. He healed them. And Jesus was pleased with the one who returned to thank Him. Use the following story to help your child retell the Bible story, using the stick puppets. You may want to put each stick in a ball of clay or play dough as stands for the puppets.

One, two, three, four, five, six, seven, eight, nine, ten. These ten men were very sick. They couldn't even live with their families. Someone in their families could get sick if they did.

One day Jesus passed near where the 10 men were. "Jesus, please help us!" they cried. Jesus stopped. He told the men to go see the priests.

On the way, the men became well. Now they could live with their families. They were very happy.

One man went back to Jesus. "Thank You for caring for me," the man said.

GCE53: Bible Story Puppets

Supplies: Copy of the finger puppet patterns and HomeLink · Cardstock or heavy paper · Scissors · Colored markers · Fabric scraps · Glue

Preparation: Make one copy of the Bible Story Puppets and cut them out. Trace them onto cardstock or heavy paper, one set for each child. Since cardstock is hard to cut, cut them out for the children before craft time. Also make a copy of the HomeLink paragraph for each child.

Directions: Give each child a set of the Bible Story Puppets to decorate. The children may glue fabric scraps on for clothing and draw facial features to make the puppets into Jesus and the Samaritan woman. Then the children can replay the story. Give each child a copy of the HomeLink paragraph to take home with their puppets.

> **HomeLink**
>
> Jesus met a woman from Samaria when she came to a well for water (John 4:4-16). She was friendless and lonely. But Jesus took time to talk with her. He told her how to find love and joy by believing in Him. Jesus cared about the lonely woman. And Jesus cares about you when you're lonely too.

GCP53: Thumbprint Picture

Supplies: Copies of the picture frame and the HomeLink · Washable inkpads · Optional: Disposable wipes · Markers or colored pencils

Preparation: Make a copy of the picture frame and HomeLink for each child. Cut them apart.

Directions: Set out inkpads, and show the children how to make a thumbprint in the middle of their picture frame. You may want to have the children clean the ink off their thumbs with a disposable wipe before continuing with the craft. Invite the children to create a picture of themselves, using the thumbprints as their faces. As the children work, talk about how each fingerprint is special to each person. In the same way, Jesus cares for each of us. When finished, have the children each glue a copy of the HomeLink to the back of their picture.

HomeLink:
John 4:4-16

Jesus cared about the lonely Samaritan woman at the well. Use the following story throughout the week to review the Bible story.

Let's go for a walk. Walk around the room. **Jesus went for a walk one day. He stopped by a well to rest.** Sit down with your child. **He asked a woman at the well for a drink of water.** She wondered why Jesus would ask her for water.

Jesus cared about the woman. He told her that He was the Savior God had promised. He told her that He could give her love and joy. The woman believed Jesus. Jesus cared about the lonely woman. Jesus cares for you too.

Jesus cares for me.
Jesus cares for me.
Jesus cares for me.
Jesus cares for me.
Jesus cares for me.
Jesus cares for me.
Jesus cares for me.